EARWIGS
TO
RHINOS

With very best wishes
Geoff Read.

EARWIGS
TO
RHINOS

Geoff Read

Illustrations by Peter Slade

Matador
9 Priory Business Park,
Wistow Road, Kibworth Beauchamp,
Leicestershire. LE8 0RX
Tel: 0116 279 2299
Email: books@troubador.co.uk
Web: www.troubador.co.uk/matador
Twitter: @matadorbooks

ISBN 978 1800464 155

British Library Cataloguing in Publication Data.
A catalogue record for this book is available from the British Library.

Printed and bound by CPI Group (UK) Ltd, Croydon, CR0 4YY
Typeset in 11pt Minion Pro by Troubador Publishing Ltd, Leicester, UK

Matador is an imprint of Troubador Publishing Ltd

This story is dedicated to my Rhino Sula,
and, of course, Sandra my wife who supported
my ramblings all the way.

xxx

Prologue

'MUM, SHAAN'S PULLED THE CURTAINS DOWN AGAIN,' shouted Aron.

'Dad, Shaan's taken an apple from the fruit bowl, and she is eating it!' called out Angie.

Trying to restore order amongst the ever-increasing chaos within our family home I grabbed Shaan and placed her on the rope climbing frame I had built underneath the table in the dining room.

Dear reader, before you contact the NSPCC please let me take you back to the very beginning where all will become clear...

I have often heard the saying 'never work with children or animals'. I obviously wasn't paying any attention as my work with animals has spanned nearly fifty years and I have fathered and nurtured four wonderful children.

From the age of nine whilst living in a poor area of South London I could be found sitting amongst rubble on the many bomb sites. In the remains of the rubble left over from the

Second World War, I looked for insects to take home and care for.

My poor mother tried hard to ignore the growing menagerie placed strategically in jars under my bed.

I knew beyond any doubt my dream in life was to work as a Zookeeper, but my teachers thought otherwise. She often told me that I was not clever enough.

That in itself is enough to deter anyone from following their dream, but especially a rather shy boy of nine years old. With the support of my mother, I never gave up, and at the age of fifteen I got my first job as junior keeper in the Insect House at London Zoo. Did I say fifteen! Yes, I only told a little fib on my application form.

Over the next almost fifty years, I worked with animals big and small, from the tiniest of insects to the largest of mammals, with some birds and big cats thrown in.

A Zookeeper's job for most days, is quite mundane. A constant routine of cleaning, feeding and poo shovelling. Regardless of the weather, rain, snow or stifling heat, animals have to be fed, watered, and cared for every day of the year, including Christmas Day.

Did I mention the reindeer? Hmm, I will later.

It all sounds quite hard work, which it certainly is, and then something happens that makes it the most amazing job.

Going into a warm animal house to find a new-born snuggled up next to its ever-attentive mother. Caring for a sick or injured animal, sometimes sitting with it all night until you notice an improvement, knowing you have done your best.

Welcoming new arrivals, sometimes from collections in foreign lands, hoping you can win their trust.

Throughout the years of everyday routine there have been many occasions that have made me laugh, made me cry and certainly made me in fear for my life.

So, why did I write this book?

When meeting someone for the first time they often ask what you did for a living. I am amazed at the interest shown when I say a Zookeeper.

I sometimes thought of saying I was a professional animal faeces removal operative but never did.

The usual question follows; *have you ever been bitten?* And when I relay some of my more painful memories of bites and injuries from the many animals I have worked with they fall into a mesmerised silence.

Did I mention the Black Widow and the feather quill? Be assured, I will.

I cannot count the times it has been said to me that I should write a book. With my teachers' affirmation ringing distant but clear in my ears, I always reply I am no academic.

As time has gone on, and with so many people telling me I ought to write a book I began to believe that maybe I could. So, it began. Armed with reams of paper to make copious notes as the memories came flooding back.

I set to work spending a lot of my time thinking of all the funny things that have happened, my mind full of the many mishaps that have beset me along the way. Then I got to thinking. Life isn't always about the funny times or the good times, of which there have been many, but also the sad times, the scary times, and times you really wish you were doing something else.

Having to say goodbye to animals that you have become so fond of over the years. The day I retired from my dream job, how could I walk away from such a huge part of my life, and many more?

With so much support from my family and evenings spent relaying all the stories from over the years, this is the finished product.

The children reminded me of so much, including the day I had to remove a window to get a chicken ark I had so lovingly built indoors, outdoors. Well, it was raining outside! Did I mention the fiasco with the chimney sweep brush? Oh, I will.

With all the reminiscing over it was down to work and with my wife providing endless cups of tea (or glasses of wine) to go with my many tantrums and *spellin mistooks* I have at last finished what I had been promising for many years. My personal account of my incredible life as a Zookeeper.

'It was never a job always a privilege.'

Acknowledgements

I WOULD LIKE TO THANK THE FOLLOWING PEOPLE WHO without their help, support, and encouragement I would still be writing the first chapter.

My long-suffering wife Sandra, for your hours at the keyboard, and belief in me.

My Agent, Editor, and close friend Tracy Willoughby who from our very first meeting has kept me on the straight and narrow, corrected my ramblings and encouraged me when I was on the point of giving up.

My children, Aron, Vincent, Angie, and Sylvia, who never lost faith and of whom I am immensely proud.

My grandchildren, Emily, my *Editor-in-Chief* who has read and reread the chapters until they made sense.

Lewis, James, Mathew, Leah, Bethany, and Summer for remembering some of the things that my old brain had long forgotten.

My very best friend and a special part of our crazy family Debbie Knight who without her help this book would never have got into print.

Peter Slade, whose artistic talents are second to none. Thank you, Peter, for the most amazing illustrations enhancing the stories I have been so keen to tell.

Peter Bircher who gave me the opportunity to go full circle and to his wife, Sue, our plant lady who taught me the importance of the plant world.

To my long-standing friend and work colleague Gaynor Worman who as well as taking time to correct my spellings and grammar has been a source of information.

Paul Irvin who has provided me with information about Marwell Zoo dating right back to its opening and beyond.

My good friend Amanda Horley, for her information on the ghosts surrounding Marwell Hall.

My first Head Keeper Bob Humphrys who cemented my career and taught me so much, also his son, David Humphreys who has always kept in touch and been a source of knowledge.

Linda Humphreys, a lifelong friend. Thank you, Linda, for the embarrassing photos of me at a young age.

My very good friend Lynne Stafford, for proof-reading my ramblings.

And to my team, in particular Simon, Dermot, Sue and Claire, who I have had the pleasure to have worked with over the years, through good times and bad we always had each other's back.

And last but certainly not least, Mr John Knowles, OBE. The man who created Marwell and gave me the opportunity to be part of such an amazing establishment. Although no longer in this world, his pioneering work in animal conservation will be long remembered.

Thank you, Mr Knowles.

The Beginning, 1966

I WAS BORN IN THE LONDON BOROUGH OF BERMONDSEY in 1950, three months premature, after the Number 1 bus my mother was travelling on towards the Elephant and Castle, suddenly hit a bump in the road disturbing me from the warmth of her body. It was then I decided to make my journey into the outside world.

A while later, weighing in at two pound two ounces and resembling a scrawny pink prawn I was a slight embarrassment to my 6ft 3in tall father.

When seeing me for the first time encased in an incubator in the premature baby unit at Guy's Hospital, my father enquired if a mix-up had occurred and that his baby was not the more robust one in the incubator next to me.

After a few weeks in hospital, I had gained enough weight to be discharged home much to the delight of my parents, Bert and Ethel.

Our home was a one-bedroom council flat on the second floor of a four-storey block. Built before the Second World

War the flats were assigned to house railway workers, my father being a train guard at the time. Later ill health forced him to retire.

Two flights of stone stairs led up to our flat; the women who lived there took turns to clean them each week. To this day I can picture my mother, a bucket of pine disinfectant next to her, her whole body bobbing up and down as she furiously scrubbed each stair until not a bit of dirt or dust remained.

Back then Bermondsey was a deprived area of South East London, slowly recovering from war-torn Britain. With a shortage of housing and high unemployment there was little money to spare. The weekly shopping bought *on tick* until pay day, when it would be paid for only to begin the same cycle all over again the following week.

The pawn brokers, often referred to as '*Aunties*', with their distinctive sign of three brass circular globes hanging over their shop doorways did a roaring trade. Most were fair, I think, though I was too young to really know. At times, the only way to make ends meet was to pawn any spare items, redeeming them if they were needed. It was the way most got by. Amid all this struggle there was a spirit of generosity, everyone in the same boat, helping each other out when they could.

Back then coal fires were the only form of heating in almost every home, central heating being only for the rich and famous. In winter thick plumes of smoke would belch out from the chimneys, blackening the sky and thickening the air, adding to the already smog-laden atmosphere.

As children we knew no different, playing out until it got dark, coming home when we were hungry, our tea a penny arrowroot biscuit, with jam, if we were lucky.

Every street was a safe place for children to play, to be adventurous, climbing walls, coming home with grazed knees, and mother applying Germolene antiseptic cream until your skin turned pink. All the children playing street games, hopscotch, knock and run and my favourite, Tin Tan Tommy, the sound of a tin can hitting a lamp post reverberating around the buildings, trying to find the other kids in their hiding places and when you did call out '*I spot Johnny behind the green lorry,*' before they beat you to the lamp post which was *Home.*

Sometimes, with a couple of friends, I would venture further afield, leaving the safety of the familiar streets to walk to Tower Bridge, taking with us a bottle of fizzy drink and a jam sandwich, knowing we would be gone all day. I remember standing on the joins where the bridge met, waiting for a bus to pass, shaking the very foundations of the pavement we were stood on. Our favourite game was climbing on the cannons, playing being soldiers, pretending to shoot cannon balls high into the air and paddling in the river Thames our feet sinking further and further into the mud and silt, until it reached our ankles, then returning home tired and hungry covered in mud.

'*Have you been paddling in the Thames again? You know it's full of germs,*' Mother would ask, a knowing look on her face.

'No, Mum,' was my reply.

'*Then how come you are covered in mud and weed?*' she would ask. That sort of gave the game away.

Like for most, the only form of heating was the coal fire in our small front room. Mother cleaned it out ceremoniously each morning, only lighting it in the evening to save on fuel. As an added bonus we also cooked great jacket potatoes in the warm ashes underneath. Retrieved from the grey dust, we would crack open the blackened, crispy skins, no jacket potato has ever tasted or smelt so good. Even now, thinking of them makes my mouth water.

Once a fortnight, the coalman, with his dirty coal dust smeared face and haggard look, would deliver two overflowing sacks of coal, up the two flights of stairs, trailing his dust-laden boots through the passage and into the front room to the coal cupboard situated next to the fireplace. The smell of coal lingered long after he had left leaving Mother to scrub the black footprints from the lino. (With pine disinfectant, of course.)

When the fire was lit the acrid but comforting smell of smoke mingled with the wafting aroma of dinner being cooked in the tiny kitchen (which also doubled as a washroom) was an interesting mix. Even more so on wash days when the floral fragrance of freshly washed sheets, hanging from a clothesline that strung across the ceiling, added to the mixture. In many houses, as in mine, that was the smell of home.

Friday was bath night. As I got older, I graduated from a good wash at the scullery sink to immersing in water in the tin bath, which was dragged from the scullery into the front room. Placed in front of the fire Mother would fill it with steaming water from the freshly boiled kettle, topping it up as the water cooled.

How I was never scalded I do not know. I was then scrubbed from top to bottom with carbolic soap, another smell I will never forget. With clean pyjamas I was sent to bed while the grown-ups bathed. Being the only-child, I was always allowed in first, followed by Father then Mother, as was the hierarchy back then.

The winter months were the hardest, when it was so cold, scraping ice off the inside of the windows to make patterns was a game. Wearing hand-knitted thick woollen jumpers that made you itch where they touched was a necessity.

At bedtime leaving the warmth of the front room to go into the freezing cold of the bedroom was hard. Hugging my arms around my body to keep warm, grateful for the hot water bottle and Father's heavy overcoat to use as an extra blanket I would snuggle as deep as the covers would allow. Every winter was the same, the dread of getting out of the bed in the morning, the hot water bottle long gone cold, testing the cold lino with one foot before racing into the front room hoping there were a few warm embers left in the fire from the night before.

Through all the times of hardship, ups and downs and growing pains, the lack of space, with just a small single bed in the corner of the only bedroom I always found room for my collection of tiny creatures, mostly kept in jam jars, some in match boxes, all kept under my bed.

As with all poor areas of London, any post-war improvements were overlooked which meant my playground was the local bomb site. Consisting mainly of dirt and rubble with small tufts of grass growing in between the long-lost buildings, unbelievably this was home to the many creepy crawlies that I was always fascinated with. The joy of finding yellow and black caterpillars of the Cinnabar moth on the ragwort plants that grew in abundance, coupled with the anticipation of what I might find lurking underneath the many stones made for some very interesting and happy times. The mixture of excitement and trepidation when, with a couple of mates, I would venture down into the old, abandoned air raid shelter, partially buried, the entrance covered in weeds and grass. Daring each other to go further into the gloom, dust, and cobwebs all around, as if entering a dark cave. Wondering what was causing the damp, musty smell. Mind conjuring up images of what we might find…A feeling of relief, tinged with a little disappointment, when the only things lurking were bits of rubble and stones was a welcome feeling.

Armed with my most treasured possessions, the *I Spy book of Insects* plus the *Observer book of Insects and Spiders*, many hours were spent at the bomb site collecting bugs of all shapes and sizes, the most interesting ones being added to my collection under my bed. Much to Mother's delight!

One of my many interests back then was the world of earwigs (they still amaze me now) however I found them very, challenging to catch, that is until I hit on, what I then thought, a brilliant idea.

Borrowing Mother's best teapot (reserved for if we had guests), Mark 1 earwig trap was invented. Buried in the ground, with top and spout visible, I sat for hours waiting and eventually watched, with trepidation, as the first earwig climbed in. I was elated; the feeling of success took hold until… it swiftly climbed back out again. Not one to be beaten and with sheer determination Mark 2 was soon in place…This time with the lid on.

All was going well and with enough earwigs to start my very own breeding programme, until... Mother discovered I had '*borrowed*' her very best teapot. After a short sharp telling-off the teapot was back in place awaiting unsuspecting guests.

Despite many setbacks the earwigs bred well in jars under my bed before I returned them back to the wild.

Although I didn't realise it at the time this was my first attempt at a captive breeding and reintroduction programme.

My passion even at an early age was to work with animals and one day after watching an episode of *Zoo Time*, a weekly television programme hosted by Desmond Morris, showing a zookeeper holding a Tarantula spider named 'Belinda', I decided there and then my future was working in the Insect House at London Zoo.

By the time I was eleven my father had died of a heart attack due to his long-term heart condition. Even as a child I realised how much our lives would change and now being 'Man of the house', it would be up to me to look after Mother as best I could.

With Mother having to manage on a meagre widow's pension of 10 shillings per week (about 50p in today's money) plus two cleaning jobs just to keep a roof over our heads and give us enough food for us not to go hungry I decided it was time for me to go to work. I managed to get an early morning milk round for our local shop, just known as Bobs.

A typical corner shop, common on most street corners, adorned with stacked shelves. A large scale used for weighing out, among other things, loose tea stood on the wooden counter. Like an Aladdin's cave Bobs sold all the essentials, loose bacon slices, wedges of yellow, orange cheese, loafs of crusty bread, all mixing with the aroma of pipe tobacco. From an array of jars, lined up as if on parade, you would find gob stoppers, rhubarb and custard, sherbet lemons, all weighed out by the ounce and put in striped paper bags. There were other sweets too, mingled together on the counter, pink mice, sherbet dippers, penny chews. I often wished I had a penny to buy one.

Each morning before school I would leave the comfort of home to walk the short distance to the shop to begin work. Carrying two wire crates full of milk bottles, one in each hand, I made my way up and down endless flights of stairs, making sure I delivered the right amount, before collecting the empty bottles, to be returned to the milk depot and sterilised to be used again. Back then recycling was a way of life.

My wages amounted to two shillings a day, the equivalent of around 10p in today's money. Although this was a small sum for the hours worked it made me feel I was contributing to the household bills and taking some of the strain off Mother's shoulders at a time when every penny was needed.

School, to me, was somewhere I had to go but never liked. The long crowded corridors filled with boys, much bigger and older than me, being pushed and bumped into, the feeling of helplessness as I made my way to the classroom. The rows of old wooden desks, the smell of stale air, pencil lead and ink from the wells all mingling together. The expectation to do well. It was all so overwhelming. All I wanted was to be outside looking under stones for the things I was really interested in.

Corporal punishment was still very prominent back then. Being hit hard over the knuckles or palm of the hand with a ruler was a common way to discipline. I remember getting three slaps on the backside with a slipper for drawing a picture of Fred Flintstone on the back cover of a bible during a rather tedious RE lesson. To this day I am unable to look at Fred Flintstone without shifting uncomfortably on my bottom.

Any ambition to work with animals was sadly not encouraged. One particular teacher, I remember to this day, telling me to *forget the idea as I was not clever enough*. I never was academic, but I knew what I wanted to do, needless to say, my attendance at school was sporadic to say the least.

By a real stroke of good fortune, I noticed an advert in the *London Evening Standard* newspaper for a keeper position in the Insect House at London Zoo, my dream job.

Although only fifteen years old and still at school, I applied, stating my age as 16. Just a small fib. Three weeks later a letter, post marked Camden Town, arrived. Fingers fumbling with excitement I opened the letter. Was this what I had been waiting for? To my utter amazement I had been invited for an interview, I couldn't tell Mother, I just couldn't.

The day finally arrived. Without telling a soul, and after much planning, akin to a secret military operation, I set off from home, walking the short journey to the bus stop, along all too familiar streets, to board the 53 bus for the journey across London to Camden Town. Over Westminster Bridge, past Trafalgar Square, surrounded by galleries and historic buildings. So many famous landmarks, not paying attention to any of them, my mind on the day ahead. My very first interview: *What if I were to fail? Am I doing the right thing? What was I thinking!*

Finally, I arrived at Camden Town and after a short walk I found myself outside the main office of the zoo. The feelings of excitement, and fear, coupled with a slight feeling of guilt for deceiving my mother made me slightly nauseous.

I nervously gave the letter to the receptionist before being directed to a small office where the interview was to be held. With one last deep breath I knocked on the door.

'*Come,*' was the command from within.

'Good morning,' I stuttered. 'I've, err, come for the interview.'

'Come and sit down, lad, don't be nervous,' said a short stocky man who I instantly recognised as the keeper holding the spider on the *Zoo Time* programme.

With books and manuscripts piled onto dusty shelves, every inch of floor space taken with more books, a faint musty smell, reminiscent of the back room of a museum hung in the air. And there, sitting behind an old wooden desk, were the men who could shape my future. Establishments officer, Mr Johns, a thin, wiry man with piercing eyes. Alongside him sat the head keeper of the Insect House, Bob Humphries.

Despite my nerves I managed to answer all the questions put to me, hoping they would be impressed with my enthusiasm. To my utter astonishment I was offered the job of junior insect keeper there and then,

'*Can you start next Monday?*' they asked. This was a Friday.

'Yes,' was my instant reply, without a thought of how!

Stunned but so happy my 53-bus journey, back home went by very quickly indeed. But then came the difficult part of telling my mother and the school.

Mother realised how serious I was and after a right telling off for deceiving her, never a good thing, she went along to the school where she told the headmaster, in no uncertain terms, I would not be returning as this *not so clever boy* has got the job he has always dreamed of. The headmaster appeared quite relieved and agreed to my leaving immediately.

Despite all those who tried to belittle my ambition, I never gave up on my dream. So, on the 4th April 1966 on a Monday morning, 2 months before my 16th birthday I started my dream job.

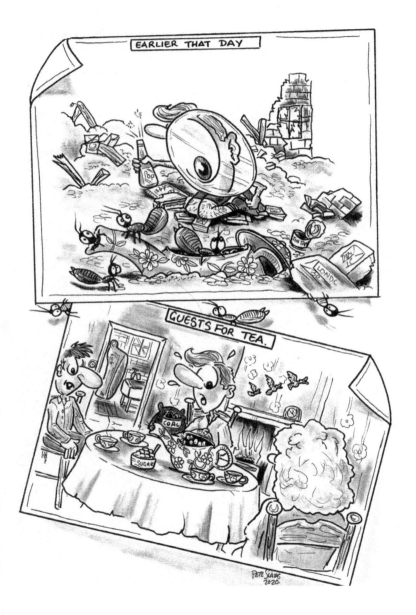

London Zoo

Waking up with the same feeling of nervous apprehension I'd had on the day of the interview I was soon ready for my first venture into the grown-up world of employment.

Following the all-too-familiar route I arrived in Camden Town to begin the short walk to the zoo with a sense of belonging, as I joined the hustle and bustle of people making their way to work, just as I was.

Before long I found myself standing outside the entrance, feelings of apprehension, nervous excitement, willing myself to go in. With time to spare I began the long walk to the Insect House. I saw the zoo with new eyes, not like a visitor or a guest, but actually as one of the staff. It was hard to believe I was there.

All around me was the noise of animals waking from their slumber. The high-pitch screech of parrots, the throaty roar of the lion, monkeys chattering like naughty children. The sound of keepers beginning their daily routine. The clang of bolts opening large metal doors, the swish of a sweeping broom, the clatter of buckets hitting the concrete floor, all of this, happening before the public descend.

At last, I arrived at the Insect House where I carefully ventured into the mess room, the place for keepers to take breaks and generally congregate. It was a medium-size room with a low ceiling; one corner was taken up by a very old-looking cream gas cooker; a large kettle was always on the boil. A chipped brown teapot, just like Mother's, took centre stage on a Formica-topped table. A worn sofa, cushions sagging to the floor from years of use, old wooden kitchen chairs, all dotted around.

The overpowering smell of bleach, carbolic soap and the harsh bronco paper in the toilet are my first, well-remembered impressions of working life.

Before long two keepers arrived; Charlie and Sid both worked in the mammal house but shared the mess room. They soon made it clear there was a hierarchy within the seating arrangements and when those immortal words, *'get out my fucking chair,'* were aimed at me, I quickly moved.

Bob soon arrived and with memories of him holding Belinda (the Tarantula spider) from the *Zoo Time* programme, I excitedly but naively thought that would be my first job of the day. Sadly, that wasn't the case.

Being *the new boy,* my duties were mainly based in the public areas, a long narrow room, resembling a corridor. Rows of tanks on either side housed a variety of insects. Spiders of all sizes. A large colony of wood ants, never still, carrying out their individual duties. Colourful beetles, centipedes, stick insects and many more.

And right at the very entrance an impressive honey-bee observation hive.

It was with a sense of pride that I carried out my daily duties of sweeping floors, cleaning the glass on all the tanks, both inside and out. Making sure everything was clean and tidy for the hundreds of visitors that climbed the old iron steps up to the entrance. Some venturing in, others not, fearful of what they might see inside the dark, dingy room.

Despite my initial disappointment that I would not be handling rare and beautiful species from my very first day I was in my element to be surrounded by all the tiny creatures I had always had a fascination with.

Part of my duty was maintaining a large butterfly and moth exhibit situated just below the main part of the insect house. A specially planted habitat to mimic as close to their natural environment plus provide a good food source had been created.

With the life cycle of a butterfly generally ranging from a month to a year it was essential to ensure a continuous display; with that in mind a quantity of butterfly pupae was regularly supplied by Robert Gooden of Worldwide Butterflies based in Dorset.

Even in the early days of conservation the Insect House was uppermost in the captive breeding of many rare species. One of the rarest species in our care was the Velvet Worm (Peripatus). With its soft worm like body and stumpy legs it was thought to be the missing link between worms and crabs. A small, but extremely important, colony was kept in a container under the table in the locust breeding room.

This provided the ideal moist, humid conditions they required for survival.

To our delight this small colony bred. What an achievement that was.

As time went on, I reached the dizzy heights of breeding all the live food mainly locusts, crickets, and bluebottle flies. These were used to feed animals on other sections as well as ours. Situated in separate buildings around the zoo each room was kept at a temperature of 33°C. causing your clothes to stick to your skin like glue. With no windows to let in natural light the cloying atmosphere made working conditions uncomfortable to say the least. When the feeding, watering and general husbandry was completed, it was time to make up the orders for the separate sections. Walking around the zoo, armed with buckets full of tasty morsels, all counted and labelled, akin to a meals on wheels delivery.

It all sounds fairly simple but believe me breeding live food is a very complex operation. As with all living creatures their habitat and care must be right, temperature, humidity, and light cycle all very important factors to ensure successful stages of development.

One of the highlights of the year was the arrival of twin brothers, John and George Newmark. They would spend their annual holidays visiting countries in Africa and India, with the sole intention of collecting species of insects and reptiles for London Zoo. Armed with shopping bags full of plastic tubs of all shapes and sizes, most unlabelled, they would arrive at the Insect House amid much excitement as to what they had in store. With all the containers carefully placed on the table, like children on Christmas morning, we would open each individual one, in anticipation of what we might find lurking inside. As this was my first encounter with these two fascinating, if a little eccentric, characters I found myself eager to join in with the excitement. I thought I would start with the smallest container, an individual ice cream tub. Thinking whatever was inside would be relatively small and harmless I removed the lid. Suddenly, without any warning as if on a spring, out jumped a huge, rusty brown King Baboon spider, front legs waving menacingly towards me, fangs out ready to strike.

'*Stunning,*' said Bob.

Frightening, I thought.

'*There are another three of those in there somewhere,*' said George.

Maybe Bob can find the others, I thought, as I slowly backed away from the table.

With all the species identified and safely put into more suitable containers the usual daily routine began. Sweeping floors was a lot safer but nowhere near as exciting.

From the age of sixteen to twenty years old, the job title for a London zookeeper was Helper. Once turned twenty-one you became an unqualified keeper.

As part of your training, you were required to study for your keeper's qualification set by Paddington Technical College in London. Despite this ruling within 6 months of starting work and at the age of just sixteen years I found myself, although officially still a Helper, promoted to second in charge of the Invertebrate section, being the one with the most experience after previous keepers had left.

This gave me a wage increase of 10 shillings or 50p a week added to my weekly wage of five pounds ten shillings and six pence, before tax. Roughly six pounds in today's money. (2020).

Despite my promotion, and the fact I would be in sole charge of the section when Bob was away, my daily routine still consisted of cleaning windows, sweeping floors, and generally tidying up however with a new staff member, Dave, joining the team I no longer had to make the tea!

Bob was due two weeks' annual leave, which meant for the first time I would be responsible for the smooth running of the Insect House, assisted by the two fairly new keepers. After endless instructions from Bob, I felt ready for the challenge.

All went well and at the end of the two weeks and with renewed confidence I was eager to show Bob what we had achieved in his absence. With all the floors swept, windows gleaming and everything clean and tidy I began to relax and awaited the praise I felt I deserved.

Until…

'Do you know what this is, Geoff?' Asked Bob

'Err, a twig,' I stuttered, feeling rather nervous seeing the look on Bob's face.

'No,' said Bob, snapping the *twig* in half. *'It's a velvet worm, a dried-up velvet worm.'*

At that very moment with the blood draining from my face and knowing I had nowhere to hide the realisation hit me that I had completely overlooked this most important species tucked away underneath the table. With heart sinking knowing I had killed the only breeding colony of this rare creature in captivity I thought I had better keep an exceptionally low profile for the remainder of the day.

Eventually Bob forgave me, maybe due to my lack of experience and my young age. I remained as second in charge, never forgetting the day I had let myself and more importantly my head keeper down. It was a hard lesson learnt and one I would never forget.

TV Debut What a Disaster

BACK IN THE 1960S LIVE ANIMALS PLAYED A PART IN many film and TV productions.

Occasionally, London Zoo would get requests for filming to take place within the zoo, mainly for factual wildlife and nature programmes. One such request arrived from Granada Television who were at the time making a documentary on honeybees as social insects. The programme was to be shown on TV for a popular weekly wildlife show called *Zoo Time*, hosted by Dr Desmond Morris.

'Do you want to be a television star?' asked Bob.

As a novice teenager of just sixteen, the first thoughts that came into my head were of fame and fortune; I was going to be a star! I imagined myself on the red carpet mingling with the rich and famous, therefore, I readily agreed. I remember Bob's advice, *'Do everything I say, no mishaps and all will be fine.'*

The day arrived and in a very public area, with cameras and sound equipment surrounding two beehives, all was set for the live outside broadcast. I was beside myself with apprehension of things to come.

All was going to plan. Bob explained how a bee colony works, how, with a complex division of labour they work together to maintain the hive, protect the queen, and produce honey.

Within a beehive is a series of stacked boxes where the honey is stored; these need to be checked regularly using, what is known as the smoking method, a device where paper is lit inside a vessel to generate smoke. Similar to bellows. My role was to smoke the top of the hive. The process alerts the bees into believing the hive is on fire therefore they start gorging as much honey as they can in case they have to evacuate the hive. With abdomens full of honey, the theory is that the bees can't bend into the shape to sting. Remember the word 'theory'.

With the live broadcast going well, a large crowd of onlookers in the public area, and with the smoker lit I began gently puffing smoke over the top of the hive.

Feeling in awe of the surroundings I misjudged the amount of smoke I was puffing and to my shock and horror, flames started appearing out of the smoker straight onto the hive. I was in danger of burning the hive down.

With one hundred plus guard bees giving off a pheromone (means of communication) to alert the other several thousand further down in the hive, I realised there could be a problem!

In no time at all angry bees were zipping through the air, their high-pitched buzzing getting louder and louder. Everything quickly started to resemble total chaos with everyone trying to escape. With heart racing I managed to back slowly away, pleased I had not been stung, unlike the camera crew, sound technician, presenter, members of the public still in the vicinity and, the most worrying of all, my head keeper!

With the area evacuated and the bees a much calmer, I began to relax a little until... I noticed a lone bee crawling up inside my protective veil.

With SAS precision it slowly crawled up onto my chin making its way to the safety of my right nostril where it settled until instinct set in and I, very foolishly, swatted it.

A piercing pain shot through my nostril radiating around my face and at once my nose started to swell. The swelling was getting bigger by the minute, resembling a bulbous mass bulging out from the side of my nose.

I slowly and painfully made my way back to the mess room where I knew Bob would be waiting for me. With little sympathy for my injury, the pain I was in, not to mention my utter embarrassment, he made it very clear I would never be asked to assist in live broadcasts again. The dream of the red carpet was definitely pulled sharply from under my feet.

Wood Ants from Burnham Beeches

O NE OF THE MOST POPULAR EXHIBITS IN THE INSECT House was a large colony of our native wood ants. Being found mainly in coniferous woodland their nests forming mounds above ground are built from a mixture of pine needles, twigs, and heather.

In the centre of the exhibit were two concrete islands, joined by a log bridge surrounded by a water moat. Ants are ingenious creatures. They frequently pushed debris into the water to form a bridge to break out, which we prevented by cleaning the moat twice daily.

Wood ants live in colonies with interlinking nests. The queen is usually deep down in the nest which meant it was very unlikely, when collecting ants from the wild, that the queen would be present. Without a queen the brood would need replenishing twice yearly to prevent the colony from dying off.

One hot summer's day, Bob and I, along with another keeper, Steve, packed the car with shovels, plastic bags, and the all-important string, to begin the journey from Regents Park to Buckinghamshire in our quest to collect fresh ants.

Away from the zoo with the countryside beckoning, work forgotten, it was just like three friends having a day out, light-hearted banter made for a happy atmosphere.

Arriving in Buckinghamshire we were soon at the entrance to Burnham Beeches, an area of ancient woodland dating back to Saxon times, where we had been given prior permission to collect the wood ants.

Following consultation with the ground staff we were shown to the site of a suitable size ant nest.

Wood ants are equipped with powerful jaws which they use for biting and immobilising their prey so protective clothing, a very fetching all-in-one, tied at the ankles with string, was essential.

Once suited and booted we, with some trepidation, started digging. The smell of damp earth and rotting vegetation was soon overpowered by the smell of formic acid which ants spray from their venom gland as a form of defence.

With Bob and I digging through the mound of twigs and leaf litter used to build the nest and with Steve holding open the bag to contain them we had soon collected enough ants to build a new colony. With many thousands of ants out of the nest, working in teams to protect their territory, climbing over our boots and up the shovel we decided it was a good time to retreat to the safety of the car.

Out of our protective clothing, slightly subdued from the many ant bites and with our eyes streaming from the acid fumes the journey home began.

Pleased with how the day had gone and with very little traffic we were confident we would be back in good time to settle the ants into their new home, until...

'Did you tie the bag properly, Steve?' asked Bob

'Of course, I did,' Steve replied, slightly put out.

'Then why are the ants loose in the car?'

One by one the ants appeared and within the confines of the car travelling at speed along the motorway it is fair to say chaos erupted. With our protective clothing securely tied into bags (which is more than I can say for the ants) we had no protection from the many incredibly angry ants that were mercilessly spraying and biting us, intent on reclaiming their territory.

After what seemed like an eternity and wondering if we would ever get out alive, we finally pulled into a service station car park where, almost before the car had stopped, we tumbled out onto safer ground, gasping in fresh air.

The sight of three grown men removing their shirts while flapping their arms about and jumping up and down on the spot may have appeared a little odd to the passers-by who deliberately gave us a very wide berth.

Sweeping as many of the ants out of the car as we could, we watched them marching along the grass verge surrounding the service station into the surrounding woodland, like soldiers on a wartime mission looking for a suitable site to build a new nest.

Finally returning to the Insect House, as three very battered, bruised and extremely embarrassed zookeepers we had the task of transferring the few remaining ants to their new home.

Over the next few days, the water moat would be regularly cleared of the debris being put in as the colony settled, hoping it would be some time before we heard those immortal words from Bob, *'We need to go to Burnham Beeches, guys.'*

Burnham Beeches Nature Reserve is now a beautiful biological Site of Special Scientific Interest and a Special Area of Conservation. The collecting of any wildlife is, quite rightly, no longer allowed.

The Bite of the Black Widow

As I had progressed in my role as second in charge, I was allowed to work with some of the more venomous creatures, one being the black widow spider, small in size but with a fearsome reputation.

Thirty of these adult spiders were kept for breeding purposes, to aid Liverpool University's anti-venom production programme as the anti-venom was unavailable in the UK at that time.

Housed in individual jars in the back room of the Insect House, a dark, dingy room with no natural light, my twice weekly task was to feed each spider with bluebottles. Unscrew lid, check spider, drop in bluebottle, replace lid. Fifteen now fed, fifteen to go, when my mind started wandering…

It's my weekend off, might take a trip to the New Forest, see if I can spot any deer. Wonder if my girlfriend, Sandra, would like to come along? I'm sure she would be impressed.

Unscrew lid, check spider, drop in bluebottle, replace lid. My thoughts continued to wander.

Must look up the train times to the New Forest. Maybe we can have a bite to eat on the way back.

Suddenly my attention was brought sharply back to task, I noticed the spider wasn't in the jar I'd just opened.

It can't have got far, was my first thought and with slight panic rising I failed to notice it had climbed on the underneath of the lid and ended up on my hand.

With a searing pain shooting from my hand and up my arm I realised I had been bitten.

Real panic set in. With fumbling hands and speed unknown to man I managed to get the spider back into the jar before racing to the mess room, heart thumping until I thought it would explode. Throwing myself through the door of the mess room, eyes wide with panic, hoping I wasn't going to lose consciousness I began babbling to Bob that I had been bitten by the Black Widow.

'*Right, Geoff, ok, calm down*,' was Bob's initial reaction until he noticed the red mark bearing the tiny puncture wounds on my hand. That was when all hell broke loose.

I could hear sirens; the ambulance lights must have been flashing as it weaved its way through, scattering the curious crowds enjoying their day out at the zoo. It arrived at the Insect House and after an initial examination I was rushed to A&E.

On arrival with my head feeling it had doubled in size and with no feeling in my left arm, I seriously thought I was about to die, I was met by every student doctor and nurse wanting to be involved in my treatment. It appeared that due to the nature of my injury I had become somewhat of a celebrity, albeit a very reluctant one.

Encased in a tiny cubicle, the sound of machinery whirring around, wondering what was going to happen to me, was I really going to die.

With the curtains closed I could hear murmurings from outside. *What were they saying? I wish someone would tell me what was happening.*

Suddenly the curtains were pulled open, an army of medics crowded around my bed. All talking at once, a barrage of questions was directed at me.

'Where does it hurt? Can you feel your arm?'

In my weakened state I could only answer a faint yes or no.

All too soon the examination began. A blunt needle was run up and down my body to measure the amount of nerve feeling as I still couldn't feel my hand or arm.

Finally, with tests completed I was left to rest with the fearful thoughts of a slow painful death running through my mind. I tried to steady my breathing in-between the invisible pain that was pounding through my head like an igniting fire radiating down my neck into my shoulder blades.

With both my arms hooked up to drips of clear liquid pain relief I soon started to feel drowsy and with the pain subsiding I gradually found myself drifting off to sleep. But not for long...

As if from nowhere more doctors with another group of students arrived, crowding into the small cubicle. Standing shoulder to shoulder, all looking down at me.

'Do you mind another examination, such an unusual case?'

Bed covers pulled back, drips in both arms and with only a thin sheet to cover my modesty. With an audience of fifteen to twenty medics, male and female, the embarrassment for me, a sixteen-year-old lad was off the scale; unfortunately worse was to come…

'*We need to test the amount of nerve feeling again,*' uttered the doctor before pulling out of his pocket… a feather quill.

Repeatedly the feather quill was run up and down my body. Did I mention my feet are ticklish? Was this a form of torture? I wondered. At last, with all tests complete I was able to rest until…

With a forceful tug the curtains were pulled open, and there stood Mother.

Armed with the obligatory bunch of grapes she marched towards me all the while giving me a stern telling off for not being more careful.

At that time there was little known regarding the treatment of venomous spider bites so having to rely on my own immune system to fight the poison I spent the next week in hospital, on a ward run with military efficiency by a very fierce-looking matron who insisted on bed sheets tucked in, everything tidy including the patients all propped up at the same angle.

At last, I was allowed home into Mother's care.

Two days after me being discharged the zoo received a telephone call to say the anti-venom would be arriving from Australia later that week. Very useful! But by then I had made a full recovery and lived to tell the tale.

To my knowledge I was the first UK keeper to be bitten by the Black Widow, not a great claim to fame but a talking point at least.

Unlike the 1960s, when there was very little in the way of health and safety legislation for invertebrates, there are now very stringent regulations relating to keeping and storing anti-venom, both in zoos and private collections.

This experience caused me to double-check every spider feed routine, not letting complacency get the better of me... or the feather quill will be waiting!

The Day I Met Dracula

DURING THE 1960S WITH DEVELOPING TECHNOLOGY at an early stage, live animals were often used on film and television sets. The popularity of horror films, particularly the Hammer Horror franchise, meant we were often asked to provide invertebrates, mainly spiders, to add scary moments to the productions.

On one occasion we were asked to provide a large bird eating spider for a film called *The Devil Rides Out*, taken from a novel written by Dennis Wheatley.

The film starred Charles Gray and my all-time favourite actor Christopher Lee.

My head keeper Bob and I decided that Belinda, a very attractive tarantula would fit the role perfectly, and as she had already starred in various TV productions her equity card was valid.

The day arrived and Belinda, Bob and I made the twenty-mile journey by taxi to Pinewood film and television studio, which was located in Buckinghamshire.

Feeling relaxed my thoughts turned to the day ahead, the excitement of being part of a film production. I wondered if I would get to meet any of the actors. I really did hope so.

What a change to the routine of sweeping floors and feeding insects.

Finally arriving at the studio, I gazed around me, in awe of my surroundings, suddenly I felt a little nervous as to what we might find inside. With no time to ponder we were met by the film's director, a tall thin man, his arms waving in all directions, he was forever on the move.

Ushering us into the building, all the while explaining what Belinda's role would be and what was expected of her (and us) before being taken onto the film set.

The set had been furnished to resemble the drawing room of an old country house. The film was set in the 1930s in London and the South of England. The scene was set for the storyline. When the Duc de Richelieu (Christopher Lee) and Rex Van Ryn (Leon Green) arrive at a party hosted by Simon Aron (Patrick Mower) they discover that it is in fact a gathering of a satanic cult, led by the High Priest Mocata (Charles Gray). The plan was to initiate Tanith, a young girl, into the cult.

On the night of the planned initiation, Duc de Richelieu and Rex Van Ryn rescue Tanith and take her to an old country mansion owned by friends. They protect themselves by sitting inside the magic circle. Under an evil spell a series of black magic attacks takes place, in order to make the group break out of the circle.

The expectation was for our tarantula, Belinda, to walk around the outside of the circle without entering it.

Tarantulas have 1000s of tiny hairs on their body and legs which are sensitive to sudden vibration and changes in air pressure; this knowledge helped us with our plan of action. Enter Bob and myself armed with a few drinking straws.

Scene set. Cameras rolling. Action…

Belinda (portrayed on film as a giant-size tarantula) enters the room, walking towards the circle edge to begin her slow walk round.

With Bob and I lying either side of her, just out of camera shot, we were able to thwart any attempt by her to enter the circle by gently blowing towards her through the straws. This encouraged her to change direction away from the inner circle.

To our amazement she kept to the script and walked serenely along the circle edge.

Her demise was to have holy water thrown over her as she crumbled and fizzled away, which we achieved by using a very realistic, dry spider skin.

All over in one take we were getting ready to leave when, to my delight, Christopher Lee, a tall, softly spoken man, came over to congratulate us and Belinda.

Was I really talking to *Dracula*? Or was it all a dream?

To this day I still have a copy of the film. Perfect!

Hero to Zero

A NORMAL WORKING DAY IN THE INSECT HOUSE, OR so we thought, until we received a rather odd telephone request asking if we could supply a quantity of bluebottles for an armchair theatre production, a series of thirty-minute plays shown weekly on ITV.

'This is one for you,' said Bob, smiling.

'No problem,' was my reply, secretly pleased, but slightly nervous, that I was to be '*in charge*'.

As part of our job was breeding bluebottles to feed the many birds and reptiles in the zoo, we had plenty to spare.

The day soon arrived and with several hundred bluebottles safely in jars and hidden in a rucksack, I was on my way, so pleased the taxi driver had no idea of the cargo I was carrying.

Arriving at Teddington studios in Greater London, I was disappointed to find a rather nondescript building not at all like I had imagined a famous film and television studio to look like. A small entrance eventually leading to a long corridor like a secret passageway with all the doors either side tightly closed. I did wonder what was behind them.

Very soon the producer's assistant arrived and took me into the studio where he gave me a very brief outline of what was expected of me, before being taken on set where a mock-up caravan was in a central position.

I felt a bit let down by the simplicity of the studio, dingy, untidy, and chaotic, everyone running around, bits of paper in hand, cables strewn across the floor, lights hanging overhead. A rather formidable lady who appeared to be shouting to herself, until I noticed she had an earpiece attached, was barking instructions to her various crew members. *Don't upset the producer*, I thought to myself.

The story line was one of a love triangle. It involved a wife, her husband and her lover with the husband accidentally being killed by the lover inside the caravan. Not knowing what to do the wife and her lover left the body locked in the caravan.

My task was to cover the body, mainly face, with bluebottles to indicate slowly decaying flesh.

To slow their metabolism down the jars of bluebottles had previously been placed in the fridge, making it easier for me to distribute them onto the body.

With so much lighting generating heat, the bluebottles would soon warm up; I would only have one take at this.

Scene set. Take one.

Actor lying on the floor inside the caravan, remains of tea and cake knocked over in the struggle.

All at once an eerie silence, nothing moving apart from the camera slowly panning up the corpse, towards his face where the bluebottles I had so carefully tipped were gradually warming up, slowly walking over his eyes, skirting across his lips, so close to his open mouth. During this time, to my utter amazement, the actor never moved a muscle and with everyone happy it was all over in the one take.

Being congratulated on 'my performance' and feeling rather pleased with myself that all had gone to plan, I began rounding up as many of the bluebottles as I could before they became too lively.

Mission accomplished I was invited to watch another scene being filmed, involving the wife and her lover embracing, a large towel covering her modesty. After all it was the late 1960s.

As they embraced, to my horror, a large escapee bluebottle flew at speed settling on top of her partially uncovered breast. Suddenly, the whole place erupted into panic, everyone rushing around like headless chickens. As the director was trying to calm a sobbing actress, I quietly made my way out of the building, leaving at least one hundred bluebottles enjoying their freedom.

I never did find out how it all ended but, apart from going from hero to villain in just a few minutes, I thoroughly enjoyed my day.

Not for the Faint-Hearted

THE SCENE IS SET. TWO COMPATRIOTS BODY LENGTH apart, sizing each other up, ready for battle. Two referees waiting anxiously for the first move. Movement from the right, then the left, slow lunge forward, arms locked together and so it begins.

No, this is not a fight to the death, but two tarantulas on a quest to mate.

My head keeper Bob and I waiting in the wings. With a piece of card in each hand to act as a shield we were poised and ready to intervene should any aggression be forthcoming.

With the female accepting the male's advances the mating ritual began.

With Bob and I on full alert counting down the minutes, one false move and it could all be over.

An eerie silence, time seemed to have stood still all around us. We were just watching and waiting.

After forty-five minutes the female started to become restless, gradually untangling herself from the male; this meant only one thing… We had to move fast, or he could be eaten.

'*Right, Geoff, don't hesitate, just do it. Quick as you can,*' said Bob.

Realising I was on my own and with a groan about to emerge from within my very soul I took a deep breath. My thoughts turned to how I was going to separate the male while he was still in the throes of trying to mate. With the female eying him up as a ready meal, packed with protein to nourish her soon-to-be-formed young I knew this was not going to be an easy task. Trying hard to steady my shaking hands knowing I only had one go at this I quickly dived in and succeeded in moving him away from the female's clutches and into the safety of a container. At least I hadn't been bitten and he was in one piece.

Like expectant fathers we waited for her to begin building her web to hold the many eggs she would produce. After several weeks, what resembled a silky cotton wool ball was perfectly formed full of tiny round eggs.

Another waiting game for the eggs to hatch, did this never end!

Counting the days until on the sixtieth day we noticed small white dots appearing inside the web. There were too many to count, all bundled together.

The excitement we felt when, after their first moult inside the sac hundreds of spiderlings began to emerge, tiny replicas of their parents.

Our next task was to remove the young, not an easy task but essential to prevent the female from eating them, then to separate the young into individual containers, to prevent them from eating each other. I did say this wasn't for the faint-hearted!

Oh, the joy I felt at the thought of feeding hundreds of individual spiderlings.

No losing concentration this time or once again the feather quill will be waiting.

As with most breeds of spiders, in particular the Black Widow, hence the name, the mating ritual often ends with the female devouring the male either before or after mating takes place. With this in mind, weeks prior to introducing the male, the female is consistently offered food, so she is, hopefully, not hungry.

Although captive breeding in zoos was relatively rare in the 1960s we, in the Insect House, devised our own programmes aimed to ensure a continuous selection of exhibits.

The Praying Mantis, their elegant beauty being an instant attraction to the public was one species we regularly bred. As if in conflict with their appearance the Mantis is in fact a voracious hunter. Their triangular head can turn 180 degrees, silently scanning the surroundings for their prey. Completely camouflaged, their incredibly strong front legs shooting out to incapacitate their prey before eating it whilst it is still alive. Female Praying Mantis have a fearful reputation of eating the male, starting first with the head, often during mating. As with our tarantulas and other species the Mantis was fed as much as possible before introducing the unsuspecting male.

In the confines of the small back room in the Insect House the scene was set for the Mantis breeding ritual to take place. This small nondescript room was fast becoming an insect den of iniquity!

Sturdy branches to hold both Mantis were centre stage and with the female placed strategically on the bottom branch all that was left was to introduce the male.

Giving her a locust to feed on, mainly to distract her while I introduced the male, I quietly placed him on the branch furthest away from her.

With her incredible eyesight she immediately spotted him. Was she interested or did she see him just as an extra food source? With no time to spare the male made his way towards the female and with no concern for his own safety jumped quickly onto her back. Still eating the locust, the female made no attempt to push him off and within minutes the mating ritually had begun.

So far, so good I thought, this could either be over within an hour or last for twelve hours. With a cup of tea for substenance, I settled down for what could have been an exceptionally long wait. With extraordinarily little natural light and the all too familiar pungent, musty smell of insects the thought of being encased in this tiny room well into the twilight hours watching two Mantis mating was not my idea of fun.

The relief I felt was tangible when, after just over an hour, it was all over and the male wishing to remain in one piece moved swiftly away to where I was able to rescue him back to the safety of his own quarters.

After two weeks the female laid an egg case holding between thirty and three hundred eggs. Within four months the nymphs started to hatch, tiny replicas of the adults, at once feeding independently.

Two weeks later the task of separating a hundred plus mantis nymphs into individual containers and then...More joy to come, feeding them every other day with tiny fruit flies. And then those dreaded words from Bob, *'Geoff, I think it's time to pair up the Black Widows,'* then, he calmly walked away.

Back then our captive breeding programmes were on a much smaller scale compared to the current conservation work carried out by zoos around the globe.

I would, however, like to think we played a small part in preserving some of the rarer species of invertebrates. I am pleased to have been a part of that.

New Beginnings, 1977

AFTER 10 AMAZING YEARS WORKING AT LONDON Zoo and now married to Sandra and having our three children, Aron, Vincent and Angela, we decided that it was time to look for pastures new.

Things had changed. London was fast becoming a rat race, the streets where I played safely as a child had become no-go areas with street gangs loitering on every corner. Doors now kept locked, the key hanging from the letter box on a piece of string long gone. The corner shops mostly replaced by the bigger supermarket chains, groceries once weighed out and put carefully into paper bags now flying down a conveyer belt, no more time to chat.

So, with my dream of wide open spaces for my children to run free I began looking for vacancies in out-of-city zoos.

An up-and-coming young zoo, Marwell, had recently opened in Hampshire, owned by Mr John Knowles, a well-known figure in the zoo world and a pioneer of conservation.

My good friend, Bill Hall, had already swapped his career as elephant keeper at London Zoo for head keeper at Marwell and recommended that I apply for a vacant head keeper position. After discussing this with Sandra and the children I applied and duly received an invitation to attend an interview.

The day of the interview soon arrived and with Sandra and three very excited children we made our way to Waterloo station to board the train to Winchester.

With the boys squabbling over who was going to have the window seat, we finally all settled to begin our journey. On a zookeeper's wage a day out by train was a very rare occurrence; that journey felt like a real adventure.

As we got further into the countryside the noise and grime of the city faded far into the distance, a patch work of colour replaced the grey of concrete. Farms were dotted about, the train rattling on past fields of cows and sheep, the boys tried to count them before they disappeared from view.

Arriving at Winchester station, with only two platforms it seemed a far cry from the hustle and bustle of Waterloo station. People walked instead of running, with time to say good morning.

Gathering together our belongings (and children), we made our way outside where our friend, Carol (Bill's wife) was waiting to drive us to the zoo, a journey of about twenty minutes.

Leaving Winchester, we found ourselves travelling slowly along country lanes. Trees either side their branches almost touching in a guard of honour. On through a small village, cottages with thatched roofs, its central point being a 700-year-old church.

The local pub with its whitewashed walls and old wooden door. A village shop, the place for local folk to gather, chat and buy essentials. My thoughts tugged sharply back to my childhood and Bobs corner shop. An old wooden hut stood in the corner of the village green; I did wonder what was inside.

Arriving at the zoo surrounded by open fields and woodland, I left Sandra and the children to take in the very unfamiliar surroundings of the countryside. The boys were playing hide-n-seek amongst the trees, a sense of freedom. Just as I had imagined.

My interview was to take place in the very stately Marwell Hall, a grand house sitting majestically at the top of the zoo, overlooking paddocks as far as the eye could see.

I was met by a member of the office staff and directed to the boardroom on the first floor and as I walked up a sweeping staircase a feeling of determination came over me. My dream of a better life for my family relied on the next few hours. I just knew I had to succeed.

I managed to settle my nerves until I was confronted by the founder of the zoo himself, Mr John Knowles. How on earth was I going to convince this very astute man I had the experience and knowledge to care for his prized possessions, when I had worked solely with creatures no bigger than my hand?

Sitting in the grandeur of the boardroom, the highly polished table, paintings on the walls of those past and present, portraits of people as well as animals.

My eyes wandered to the view from the window, large open paddocks, Zebras frolicking around, the magnificent Ostrich making his presence known.

Trying hard to remember all I had learnt from my two keeper's courses, hoping Mr Knowles would put my stuttering and stumbling down to nerves, I tried to answer all the questions to the best of my ability, adding my thoughts that all species require the best quality of husbandry and respect and in my opinion, you should never stop learning about the animals in your care.

With the interview over Mr Knowles and I met with Sandra and the children for a tour of the zoo. Clambering into his battered old Land Rover, the sound of its exhaust could be heard for miles around, the children thought they were on an adventure safari.

Past more paddocks, Scimitar-horned Oryx, the emblem of Marwell, with so much space to roam freely, how different from a city zoo. Past the Tiger enclosure. Such magnificent cats sleeping peacefully, but always with one eye open.

The final leg of our journey was to the Snow Leopard house to meet 'Vilkku' a stunning female cat who greeted us with a deep purr, rubbing her face along the mesh.

'What are your thoughts on the vacant position, Geoff?' asked Mr Knowles.

With so much to take in and nerves forgotten I replied, with great enthusiasm, how much I would love the job but appreciated he had other candidates to interview.

Much to my surprise, with a shake of the hand, he offered me the position of head keeper with a starting date of four weeks' time.

Part of the package as head keeper was rent-free accommodation by way of a 3-bedroom cottage, backing on to woodland which separated it from the zoo's perimeter fence. Almost as an afterthought we were given a very quick viewing, mainly I think to prevent us noticing the holes in the floorboards and the broken stair banister, but that aside the cottage seemed perfect for us. Secluded down a country lane, surrounded by woodland the boys were already planning the building of their first den.

It was soon time to head back to the station for our journey home. Everyone talking at once about our new adventure. The children unable to sit still, buzzing with excitement.

The very next day, back home and with reality setting in, we began making plans for our move to the country. Telling family and friends was easy; they respected what a great opportunity this was for us all. My one dread was telling Bob Humphries my head keeper at London, who after the initial shock was very understanding and respected my decision. He was always an inspiration to me and taught me so much, cementing my zoo career.

With help from close family the daunting task of packing up our possessions and moving out of our two-bedroom council flat was soon completed.

With our good friend Steven driving a hired removal van, Sandra and I squashed together on the passenger seat and the children sitting securely amongst the furniture in the back, we were on our way.

Leaving London behind us we were soon heading into the countryside. Lush green fields, wide open spaces, the grime of crowded London streets a distant memory.

Before long we found ourselves loading our meagre belongings into our new home, treading carefully around the broken floorboards. It was a typical estate workers cottage, empty and unloved but with a wealth of history within its hundred-year-old walls. The lounge with its open fire, the cupboard under the stairs, perfect for a game of hide-n-seek. The kitchen, its walls old and crumbling. In centre stage an old blackened range, waiting to be brought back to life. We discovered what looked like a cupboard, but on closer examination turned out to be a tiny bathroom. With just three bedrooms upstairs it was not long before our furniture was in its rightful place. With the beds made it was time to tackle the lighting of the fire. I tried to remember how Mother used to do it.

Rolled up newspaper placed strategically on the bottom, a few sticks of kindling and last, but not least, a meagre amount of coal. *Easy,* I thought, until... To my dismay I realised the birds had been using the empty chimney for nest building.

With the room filling up with smoke, all the windows open, I wondered how long it would take the fire brigade to find us. With a great whoosh the burnt remains of the nest tumbled down into the grate, unblocking the chimney.

Well, that wasn't too bad, I thought, until I saw the blackened mess on the floor and the look on Sandra's face. With the day drawing to a close, and the fire burning nicely in the grate, night-time was fast approaching. The inky blackness of the countryside was something we had never experienced before. The ghostly shapes of the surrounding trees, the night sky alive with millions of stars; the boys trying to identify the planets until the warmth and safety of the cottage beckoned us back inside. With the children tucked up in bed, and the wine opened, Sandra and I relaxed in front of the fire watching the flickering flames turning from orange to red, the aroma of burning logs filling the air. All at once a feeling of contentment washed over me. No longer was the cottage empty and unloved, it was now our home.

I was due to begin my new post the following Monday therefore I had just two full days to contribute to finishing the unpacking and arranging furniture. Much to Sandra's delight Monday soon arrived and she was able to complete the task unhindered.

The next step was to enrol our sons, Aron and Vincent, in their new school, Owslebury infants and junior school in the village which was three miles away.

After being part of a multi-cultural, intercity school where the classroom size was thirty plus it was quite a shock to arrive at a school with fifteen pupils to a class.

Aron told me some time later he thought the rest of the children were away on holiday.

On their first day the class was tasked with creating a pond in the newly acquired nature garden. Both boys, although enjoying their new learning regime found the first few months difficult to settle. A much slower pace of life, no corridors full of children rushing to be first in class. Everything was so different. Very soon they began to make friends, inviting them home to play in their newly built den or as a special treat to be taken to the zoo in the evening when it was closed to the public. What an adventure for young boys to have a zoo as their playground. Life couldn't have been more different.

As time went on, we became accustomed to village life, joining in the many activities open to us including the much-loved drama group. The whole family took part in the annual village pantomime where, for many years, I was type cast as the Dame, adorned in very fetching pantomime frocks, bright red lipstick and the biggest bra that could be *borrowed* from a lady living in the village. Anonymously, of course!

First Day at Marwell, May 1977

L ONG BEFORE THE ALARM WAS DUE TO GO OFF AT 6AM, I was woken from a deep sleep by an unfamiliar sound. *What's that noise? Is that a tiger roaring?* Still thinking I was dreaming, I got out of the comfort and warmth of my bed and, in a vain attempt not to wake the whole household, made my way gingerly down the stairs. I tried not to step on every creaking stair and floorboard. Then came that noise again. Still half asleep, my mind in a blur until I remembered I now lived in a zoo and, yes, it was indeed tigers roaring.

Sitting alone in the lounge the remaining embers from last night's fire faintly glowing in the hearth I wondered what the day would bring. My thoughts wandered. *Had I made the right decision uprooting my family to bring them to a newly opened zoo without the security they were so familiar with?*

Trying to banish the maudlin thoughts going round in my head I quietly closed the door behind me and left the warmth of the cottage to embark on the first day of my new career.

I began the ten-minute commute to work, through a field, the grass awash with early morning dew, before entering a bridle way for the remainder of the journey.

With the earthy smell of rotting wood, trees either side reaching out with their gnarled branches, perfectly formed spider webs glistening in dappled light, I marvelled at the variety of wildlife accompanying me on my way to work. A lone squirrel raced up and down a tree, darting back and forth as if playing peek-a-boo, the chorus of birdsong, each one different, but singing in unison. What a change it was from the jam-packed streets of London.

In no time at all I had arrived at the zoo entrance, just a gateway with one kiosk for the public to pay their admission fee.

Waiting for me was the Assistant Curator, Joe Haddock who I had previously known from my days at London Zoo. A tall, slim man with an air of elegance about him in contrast to his rather quirky character.

'Time for a tour of the zoo and to meet the other keepers,' said Joe, handing me a set of keys which unlocked every animal cage throughout the zoo, and a Hackney Thunderer referee's whistle. *'Should you encounter any escapes,'* he mentioned, almost as an afterthought. I wondered if he meant should I cause any escapes.

Just like my first day at London Zoo, I was a little apprehensive at meeting my fellow keepers, I felt a bit like a little fish in a big pond after the confines of the Insect House. But I was so determined to make a success of my new job in this strange but wonderful environment.

It was finally time to meet my own section keepers, Sue and Dermot, both with much more experience than me in looking after larger animals. As I walked towards them, I wondered how they would feel towards a head keeper who had only looked after insects. Would they share their knowledge with me, or would they resent me for the position I held? How on earth was I going to live up to their expectations?

I really need not have worried as with a smile and a handshake they were both friendly and welcoming.

Back then the zoo was split into three sections. The North section with herd animals suited to vast open paddocks. Antelopes, Zebras, all with space to roam.

The bird section, smaller with individual aviaries was home to parrots, and many breeds of pheasant. The larger flightless birds, the magnificent Ostrich and smaller Rheas sharing paddocks with the herd animals. All blending together.

South section, my domain, aptly named South Road, consisted of a long narrow road flanked by woodland with enclosures on either side housing a variety of animals from many corners of the world: Brazilian Tapirs, Kangaroos, and Kudu.

Enclosures housing the smaller breeds of cats, Cheetahs, Serval and Lynx, to name but a few.

The Children's Zoo, also part of the South section, was a small area that housed several domestic animals, including rabbits, guinea pigs, and pygmy goats and my non-favourite animal, the donkey. The one exception to the other more pet-like animals was a rather handsome European wild boar, found wandering along a country lane in Odiham, a small village in North Hampshire. He was brought to the zoo for safe keeping.

The keepers named him Caulston after the local village policeman. We never did find out if he was aware of this.

Completing my section was the stableyard, part of the walled garden of Marwell Hall. An impressive stone-built area which still had remnants of times long past, when as a kitchen garden an abundance of fruit and vegetables would have been grown to feed the Lord and Lady of the house. During my time as head keeper this area was used as a quarantine area for new or sick animals.

There was little time for socialising, it was down to work, animals don't take kindly to be kept waiting for their feed.

Dermot and I set off to start the day's work.

First job of the day cleans out the European bison, a giant of an animal who can reach over six feet in height and weigh 2,000lbs but which is also extremely agile and capable of jumping a three-metre-wide stream from a standing position. They are also known to attack when provoked.

Determined not to be fazed by the sheer magnitude of my first encounter with these magnificent beasts, I followed Dermot into the house which I can only describe as basic, little more than a shed with reinforced walls and a gap where a door should have been. The sweet aroma of hay and animal firmly encased within the confines of the walls, lingered on my clothes long after I had left.

Wondering how on earth we were going to shut the animals out while cleaning inside, Dermot handed me a long metal pole. *Interesting,* I thought.

The female Bison, aptly named 'Bitch', seemed happy to walk out of the house to the outside paddock.

Well, that was easy, I thought to myself; *don't know what all the fuss was about.* How wrong I was!

To prevent her coming back in the metal pole had to be slid across to secure the opening. We had 8-10 seconds to do this before, with nostrils flaring, Bitch turned and ran back at us.

The ground shook as she stormed towards us, her huge head, and curved horns ready to inflict serious injury, bracing myself for the impact until…She suddenly stopped, just short of the doorway, and wandered away as if nothing had happened.

With renewed respect for this magnificent beast, I realised she was just showing her dominance and obviously knew the routine as much as we, her keepers, did.

Once my heart rate had returned to something close to normal, we carried on with the task in hand. I was very pleased to have Dermot with me although I did detect a wry smile for the newbie.

What a baptism of fire, locusts were so much easier.

My first challenge over I felt ready to face whatever else was to be thrown at me that day, or so I thought, until that is, I encountered the Guanacos, native to South America and part of the Camel, Llama and Alpaca family.

They were housed in a large paddock which they shared with a herd of Greater Kudu, a large Antelope from South Africa. With the Guanacos having access to the paddock at night and the Greater Kudu during the day every morning two keepers, armed with a broom each for protection, would try to persuade the Guanacos back into the house to enable the Kudu to be let out into the paddock.

'Watch out for Gob-Gob, our dominant male,' said Dermot. Was that another wry smile I detected?

Guanacos are generally mild-mannered creatures but, when showing dominance, they can spit to a distance of up to six feet. Gob-Gob the lead male, with his long legs and thick neck, was no exception, hence the name, which I discovered to my dismay. He continuously spat over us until we reached the house where a fresh bed of straw awaited him. As we shut the gate behind us it was the perfect moment for him to eject an extraordinarily large spit of powerful-smelling pre-digested grass.

I knew long before I accepted the post at Marwell that large animal husbandry was a messy, dirty job, out in all weathers, wading about in mud and worse, cold seeping deep within your bones. Even a long soak in a hot bath couldn't alleviate the very distinctive smell of hay, straw, and animal but I had never come across anything as pungent as the smell of Guanaco spit. What an initiation.

Guanaco safely shut in their quarters and with me smelling like a compost heap, and with little time to draw breath, it was on to the Greater Kudus, our next job of the day.

With the Kudus safely in the paddock the routine of cleaning out the old bedding and replacing it with fresh was relatively easy, if not physically challenging.

Time to build up some muscles, I thought.

With the morning routine finished it was time to head up to Treetops restaurant for lunch. Following Dermot up a very steep hill we finally reached the top where the welcome aroma of cooking awaited us. Chips with everything, but all

I really wanted was a cup of tea after the morning's hard work.

Walking into the restaurant where the keepers were congregated was like walking into the mess room on my first day at London Zoo. Finding somewhere to sit I waited for those immortal words... 'Get out my fucking chair.' Instead, I was greeted with handshakes and introductions and a free cup of tea. I was really beginning to feel that I belonged.

With lunch over it was time to prepare the evening feeds for the animals. Chopping the never-ending pile of apples, carrots, cabbages and bananas, all different shapes to be cut into the right size for each individual animal. Learning about the various pelleted food, trying to take in all that Sue and Dermot were explaining to me. Different feed for different species. So much easier to drop a few flies into a jar.

My head felt like it was about to burst with so much information to take in.

Was it ever going to end?

The remainder of the day went very quickly and soon it was time to feed, check and settle the animals for the night.

First the Kudu who with the promise of food and a fresh bed of straw made their way to their sleeping quarters. The male first, followed by his harem of females.

As I said the animals knew the routine as well as we did.

With a feeling of impending doom, I realised our next job was to let the Guanacos out and with the thought of Guanaco spit uppermost in my mind, I opened the gate.

Standing well back, hoping Gob-Gob's aim was not far reaching, I was so relieved when he walked calmly out of the house where the promise of fresh grass awaited him. Just when I thought I was safe, Gob-Gob had other ideas and as I reached over to close the gate behind him, he threw his head forward to release a torrent of pre-digested hay. I realised without doubt that I would need more than a pair of tweezers to care for the animals in my charge.

Back then there was no official closing time with the working day finishing when the last member of the public had left. Thanking my team members for looking after the newbie so well and with the sun setting, I made my way back home, through the bridle way, the trees looking a little more menacing in the dappled evening light. The birdsong was fading as dusk started to fall.

As the lights of the cottage came within sight, I wondered what reception I would get when Sandra discovered my uniform had to be washed, dried, and ironed in time for work the very next day, without the luxury of a washing machine or tumble dryer. I had a niggling feeling in the back of my mind this would not go down too well.

I arrived Safely home, to be greeted by a chorus of… *What is that smell?*

The sight of the children huddled around the log fire, holding their noses, waiting to hear about my adventures. The aroma of cooking wafting from the kitchen.

Sandra starting to run me a bath. It was at that precise moment I knew, without a shadow of a doubt, I had made the right decision for us all. So, begun our new, amazing life in the country.

The Day of the Wombat

'GEOFF, WE ARE GETTING A WOMBAT TO LOOK AFTER, do you know anything about them?' said Mr Knowles.

I mumbled something resembling, 'Yes a bit, probably.' At the same time thinking, I hope he doesn't ask me what I know about them.

'Tell me what you know about them,' he asked.

'Where do you think it could go?' I asked, quickly changing the subject, hoping he hadn't noticed.

With that Mr Knowles got out of his pocket a crumpled cigarette packet and drew on it what resembled a plan; it consisted of just a fence and a gate. With no time to spare I identified a suitable area and work began.

Wombats have a tough, barrel-shaped body, with short powerful legs, and long claws. Being a muscular animal, they are adept at digging through soil and stones.

With that in mind the area was filled with shingle and with fencing (and a gate) in place. The Wombat arrived.

After reading up on everything known to mankind about Wombats, I felt sufficiently prepared to enter the enclosure, armed with bucket and broom ready for the daily task of poo clearing. An interesting fact is that Wombat poo is square shaped. It is believed they defecate to mark their territory. They have special bones in their backside that forms the poo into cubes, preventing it from rolling away.

Once in the enclosure and ready to start work, the Wombat suddenly came at me, ferociously attacking my feet and ankles as I made a hasty exit to safety.

Plan B had to be thought of quickly before the zoo opened and I had the public as an audience.

Looking around the back of the enclosure I found an old abandoned rusty metal dustbin. I made sure no one was looking and quickly jumped into it, kicking out the base. Now for the moment of truth. Holding onto the handles, broom and bucket balanced, I shuffled into the enclosure, closely resembling a Dalek. Resisting the urge to say, 'We will exterminate,' the performance began.

Dustbin down, sweep, dustbin up, shuffle... Dustbin down, sweep, dustbin up shuffle and repeat. With the Wombat continuing the attack, trying hard to reach my ankles through the dustbin, I gradually shuffled my way around the enclosure and out of the gate.

Congratulating myself on my success, thinking that I had got away with that without being seen, I had failed to notice Mr Knowles had driven up to see how his Wombat was settling into the new routine. Shaking his head in painful disbelief at the sight of his new head keeper dressed as a Dalek being attacked by a Wombat he slowly drove away.

At that point I did wonder just how short-lived my career at Marwell was going to be!

Roo Rearing

WHAT STARTED AS NORMAL WORKING DAY, IF THERE ever was such a thing in a zookeeper's life, turned out to be, a bit different by the end of it.

The daily routine of checking and cleaning our charges began as usual.

Soon it was the turn of the Kangaroo group consisting of one male and four females, which we hoped was a good ratio for breeding.

When you enter any animal enclosure it's good practice to talk to the animals to let them know you are about to enter their domain, but the male, being a big lad weighing at least 50 kg, ignored any attempt at conversation and was always the first to challenge me. By leaning back on his very muscular tail he would pull himself up to full height, which was nearly 2 metres, and to show his dominance would flick his penis out and pee at me. Although never a good shot I think I know what he would be saying if he could speak, and the message was sent and received very clearly.

With cleaning finished I was about to leave the Kangaroo house when something in one of the corners caught my attention. On further investigation I discovered a wrinkled, pink Joey (Joey being the term for a baby Kangaroo) far too small to be out of the pouch. Thinking it was dead I picked it up and placed it gently in my pocket when suddenly I felt movement; at that moment I made the bold decision to give it a fighting chance by having a go at hand rearing it.

The main challenge was feeding it the right formula. With a Kangaroo's milk being very high in protein and thick in consistency, the only way the little Joey was going to stand any chance was by me finding some way of replicating it. After many trials, a mixture of goat's milk and tinned Carnation Milk was devised and with the smallest animal teats we could find. Within two hours of rescue the feeding routine had begun.

Young Kangaroos rely on their mother's body heat for warmth; they also need to feel movement so with that in mind my wife, Sandra, made a 'pouch' out of a baby's blanket folded in half with ties to go around the waist of whichever family member was closest and available. The first couple of days went by without a hitch until we needed a fresh supply of Carnation Milk and with everyone else out, it was left to Sandra. With Joey safely tucked in the pouch she made the twenty-minute journey to the local supermarket.

Weaving through the crowds of shoppers with their overloaded trolleys Sandra quickly made her way to the tinned produce and grabbed the all-important Carnation Milk before joining the snaking queue to the checkout. Feeling a little warm Sandra carefully unzipped her jacket to cool down trying hard not to disturb the sleeping Joey. With the shopping moving swiftly along the conveyer belt to the tune of the barcode scanner, a tired-looking cashier wishing her workday over; it was just the packing to complete... And relax...until...In the blink of an eye a very pink, wrinkly Joey popped her head out of the pouch looking directly at the cashier before, what seemed like an eternity, she popped her head back down. Not a word was spoken, and with transaction completed, goods packed and paid for, Sandra made a very quick exit out of the store, leaving a bewildered and possibly traumatised cashier wondering if she had imagined the whole thing.

If you ever watch an episode of the TV series *Fawlty Towers* called 'The Hotel Inspector', the scene with the biscuit tin and the rat will come close to that experience.

Our attempt to raise our little Joey came to an end when, after nine days, she passed away. Like many animals the mother knows best, and on occasion babies are abandoned. Quite frequently the intervention and hand rearing process work to give the new-born that extra TLC needed, but sadly not on this occasion, the parent of that little Joey seemed to possibly sense the chances of its survival were minimal. Mum's maternal instinct knew she could not survive which was the probable reason for her being abandoned.

Wounded by a Bird

'THE CASSOWARY HAS AN INFECTED SWOLLEN MIDDLE toe,' I reported to the curator.

'*Vet's due in tomorrow, we'll get him to check it,*' was the reply.

Cassowaries are a magnificent flightless bird from New Guinea, said to be the most direct descendant of dinosaurs. Aggressive by nature, they can weigh up to 60kg and standing almost 2metres tall they look like a cross between an Ostrich and a Turkey.

They are capable of inflicting serious injury using their casque, a helmet-like hollow structure located on top of the head, plus their dagger-like middle claw, they are not a bird to mess with.

The day of the vet's visit started like any other, routine checks on other animals completed, it was then the turn of the Cassowary. A thorough examination of the toe was required and with the Cassowary being sedated and after checking very cautiously that she was asleep, the work began. Without warning she had a spasmodic reaction, an extremely common after-effect of some sedation drugs. With a powerful kick of her leg the middle claw caught my finger.

After a few choice words, like *goodness me that hurt'*, I tentatively looked to discover my index finger had been slashed open, revealing the bone. Lucky enough the vet was on hand to administer first aid before I was quickly rushed off to A&E.

Still in Zoo uniform with my finger dripping blood my arrival caused quite a stir amongst the medics and patients alike.

Word soon got around that a zookeeper was in who says he's been *kicked by a bird* and as I recalled the story painful memories of the bite of the black widow, and the never-to-be-forgotten quill feather came racing back into my mind.

Encased in a tiny cubicle, medics surrounding me, all wanting to examine the deep, gaping wound caused by a... *Bird*.

Finally, examinations complete, wound cleaned and stitched I was allowed home to be fussed over by Sandra and the children and given a well-deserved cup of tea, the great British cure for all dramas.

Next day back to work. With a finger bandage resembling Mount Everest and a very impressive arm sling, I carried out whatever routine I could manage with one hand.

Four days on with the finger still very painful, starting to swell and turning a very strange colour, it was back to A&E.

With the diagnosis that it was very infected passed on by the Cassowary, the stitches had to be removed, the wound once again flushed through and a very tight dressing applied.

With antibiotics prescribed it was back home for more sympathy and yet another cup of tea.

It took a few weeks and two further courses of antibiotics before the infection cleared. Despite the wound healing my finger was badly scarred impacting upon my ability to completely straighten it.

On the advice of Peter, the curator, and with the full backing of Mr Knowles, the decision to try to claim compensation was made. Although reluctant to do this as, in my mind, it was an accident with no one being at fault, Peter assured me the zoo had the relevant insurance to cover any such claim.

As part of the claim process, I was summonsed to attend an assessment. On arrival I was shown into a room where three very stern-looking gentlemen sat behind a desk. Feeling uncomfortable and slightly nervous I explained the difficulties I was facing as a direct result of the injury. I was finding it difficult to hold a broom, essential in my line of work. It was also affecting my training in Aikido, a Japanese martial art; many of the techniques used were reliant on hand movements and grip. I could no longer wear my wedding ring due to the pain from the scarring, a factor which did upset me.

'*No divorce on the cards then,*' said one of the assessors, a wry smile on his face.

At last, some humour.

After more questions it was time for a physical examination of my finger and then, without warning, I was asked to remove my shirt. This seems very odd, I thought, until I realised it was to test my finger dexterity while doing up buttons.

With the assessment over, one by one the assessors shook my hand; I believe they wanted to see if I could really not grip with that finger.

A month or so later a letter arrived approving my claim and informing me I was now officially one percent disabled and awarding me £90 in compensation!

Rodeo Roundup

A s with all living creatures, regular health checks are advisable, with this in mind every year the animals, in my case Bennett's Wallabies, Flamingos and Rheas would be given a thorough health check, after all they couldn't tell us when something was wrong; our keen eye and expertise and regular check-ups were essential.

When the curator said those daunting but necessary words, '*it's time to round up the Wallabies, Geoff,*' anxiety set in with what was in store.

First things first, assemble the team together in preparation to be out run, bitten, kicked, and generally pooed on.

Our first job was to catch the Wallabies, not an easy task I might add, particularly as they had the run of a rather large area named Wallaby wood, complete with a path for the public to walk through.

As well as checking the health of each individual animal it was an opportunity to look to see if there were any Joeys in the pouch and to determine the sex of any out of the pouch.

Sounds simple I hear you say... Let me give you a little instruction to the task. First you must catch your Wallaby by the base of the tail, lift it high, check the pouch, and mark with a colour spray and release.

Did I say simple?

With over twenty Wallabies, each weighing up to eighteen kilos, running at speeds of twenty-five mile per hour and capable of jumping two metres.

What could possibly go wrong?

With four keepers at the ready it was fairly easy at first to catch each Wallaby in turn, but as the numbers dwindled and with the Wallabies (and keepers) running in different directions it became harder to differentiate which ones had been caught and which ones hadn't even after being sprayed.

Just like Kangaroos, Wallabies have extremely powerful back legs, automatically kicking out, but providing we all kept a fair distance from their aim all should be well.

My first capture, a young female with no Joey in pouch proved relatively easy as was the next one, a young male, sprightly but again no problem.

Well, this is going well I thought as I grabbed a rather large male and lifted him up.

How I wish I hadn't! With a well-aimed kick, he caught me where it really does hurt, how I wished I had worn a cricket box.

With a rather loud yelp I let go of the Wallaby before falling with an almighty thud to the ground.

Lying in agony, not daring to move I noticed my keepers showing massive concern. They were making strange choking noises, their faces were hidden, and their hands held firmly over their mouths. They must have been hoping I wouldn't be upset to see the tears streaming down their faces. How touching that they are so concerned for me, I thought. Concerned, or suppressing hysteria? I now ask myself.

After staggering back to the mess room, whilst closely resembling the Ministry of Silly Walks, I checked all was well and returned to my *oh so caring* team where I took over the clip board to record the data collected. Surprisingly, I stayed as far away from the Wallabies as I could.

I was very thankful when the task was completed, however my relief was short-lived as the same thing happened again the following year, and the year after that!

Would I ever learn?

A week later it was the turn of the Rheas, a flightless bird from South America who also had to be caught and checked for any foot problems they may have encountered and to identify any mite infestation.

A flightless bird you may think would be easy, it certainly is not! Standing well over a metre high, weighing around 30 kilo and capable of running at over thirty-five mph, all the while turning and swerving like rugby players eager to get to the touch line. Not the easiest to catch to say the least!

With six straw bales in place to act as an examination table we were ready to begin. Two keepers to catch the bird, holding a wing each, while running as fast as possible all the while trying to keep up with the bird's speed, not giving it the opportunity to stop and lash out with its large powerful legs and feet or its dagger-like claws capable of slashing the thickest of skins. Like many of our tasks, only for the fittest!

Once held safely and firmly on the straw bales, my task was to check the feet and wings before spraying the underneath of each wing with mite repellent.

Once complete, and again with a wing each, the bird would run us all the way back to the paddock where another fifteen to eighteen birds would be waiting. So, then for it all to begin again. That year shattered but injury free I was very thankful it was over, for another year at least.

Before the arrival of springtime and with it the chance of strong winds forecast, it was necessary to catch and check our flock of Flamingos. As with the Rheas they are prone to foot problems, the most serious being bumble foot, a bacterial infection common in captive Flamingos and awfully hard to treat, making this particular health check extremely important.

All captive Flamingos are pinioned, which means their wings are clipped to prevent them from flying away, however, with a gentle breeze ours could lift themselves off the ground to a height of ten feet. To combat this and with no harm to the bird we would carefully cut away a few primary feathers.

With Flamingos being such delicate birds, a much softer approach was required so the health check was being carried out within their own inside quarters.

To minimise any stress to the birds, three keepers would be in attendance, quietly talking while the first bird was caught, and with a long-practised technique it would be gently held around the body, head facing backwards and with its delicate legs held outstretched making it easy to check the feet.

With no powerful legs and sharp claws to contend with the only thing we had to watch out for were their long necks. At the end of such long, delicate necks are very sharp beaks, just right for nibbling you with. Starting at my ears before moving on to my neck they would nibble away, and with both my hands holding firmly onto the bird there was very little I could do to stop it.

With all the birds checked the only thing left to do was wait until the skin around my neck and ears grew back, just in time for the next roundup.

Despite my injuries accrued during this time I knew the yearly round check-ups were a very necessary and important part of animal husbandry and care, identifying and treating any problems at an early stage paramount to their constant care.

I never did buy a cricket box… I just delegated instead.

Almost the Great Escape

'Geoff, we have a pair of rare Asiatic lions arriving from a zoo in Germany,' said an extremely excited Mr Knowles.

Knowing there were only a few hundred left in the wild, their last remaining habitat being the Gir Forest in India, I realised the importance of this conservation species.

Part of the South Road section included a flint-walled stable yard, converted into holding areas for new arrivals and quarantine facilities. With one of the larger pens having two indoor quarters, both with a raised wooden bed board, and separated by a heavy slide, it would make ideal accommodation while waiting for completion of a new lion house.

The day of the lion's arrival came and with the first large crate in position all was going well.

Slide up; the female hesitantly looked all around, before slowly walking into the indoor quarter, slide gently lowered. The same procedure for the male who, although not as calm as the female, eventually made his way inside.

After we gave them a few hours to settle I quietly made

my way back to check on them both. First the female, where, to my utter horror and disbelief the bed board was empty. With my mind in turmoil, I began questioning what my eyes could clearly see. *Where was the female? Has she escaped? How did she escape?*

Adrenalin pumping through my body, trying hard to remember how to breathe while waiting for common sense to catch up. *She really could not have got out, could she?* Then, a feeling of total relief on catching a glimpse of a large paw poking out from underneath the raised bed board.

With breathing back to normal but still on high alert, I made my way to check on the male who, I was so pleased to see, was calmly resting. My relief, however, was short-lived when, without warning, he pounced, and with a sudden roar, making the ground beneath me shake, he attacked the wire mesh door with such force I seriously thought it would break. Thinking that was probably a good time to leave I quietly, but a little shakily, made my way out.

Next morning a check on our new arrivals found the female resting quietly, this time on top of the bed board.

Hoping this would be the same with the male, but feeling somewhat apprehensive, I quietly looked in on him, to be greeted with ears back, snarling, razor-sharp canine teeth showing ready to launch himself at me, his prey. Maybe he is still settling in, I thought.

After a few days, taking into consideration they had been together at their previous zoo, we thought it safe to let them out to explore the outside area.

All appeared well as they greeted each other with a head rub, until… The male saw me.

With a thunderous roar he leapt at the wire, you could smell the aggression, he really wanted to hurt me.

This continued every day regardless of my gentle approach to him. Feeling sad that he seemed to have taken an instant dislike to me I knew there was very little I could do, he was, after all, a wild animal.

The following week the vet was due to carry out a routine health check on both animals. My task was to separate them into their individual living quarters where they would be sedated for the vet to carry out a thorough health check. After several unsuccessful attempts I left them both together in the male's quarters thinking I would try again after lunch.

On my return, back on section I was surprised to see the vet and several other keepers gathered around a sedated male lion.

'How did you manage to separate them?' I asked.

There was a deathly silence before my very astute friend Bill, gave me a look that only said one thing… *We need to get out of here.*

'Can we all very slowly back out,' I quietly uttered. With the only sound being our collective heartbeats. We all did as I had asked.

Assuming I had separated the animals before lunch and with the vet arriving early to find the male on his own it was deemed safe to begin. With the male sedated and the health check underway no one realised the female was underneath the bed board, no doubt quietly eyeing up whose legs looked the tastiest.

With lessons learned in communication and the female

safely back in her own quarters the health check was completed much to everyone's relief.

As time moved on their new accommodation was complete, a good-size house with four internal connecting dens. A large grassed outside area, divided in two, with regulation-height fencing and wire overhang made the exhibit safe as well as look attractive and spacious.

The day of the move went well, and both settled into their new quarters quickly, but still the sight of me produced anger from the male.

With just woodland between our cottage and the new lion house, the sound of him roaring in the early hours of the morning, impressive as it was, did sound a bit like '*Geoff, Geoff, Geoff!!!*'

Almost the Great Escape Part 2

ONE PARTICULAR DAY WHILE ON MY WAY HOME FOR lunch, a member of the public passed me and casually said, 'Hey mate, your lion's getting out.'

'Cheers,' I replied. Smiling politely, I carried on home. Our wonderful public do say some funny things.

Almost at the gate, ready by now for my lunch, a very flustered, red-faced lady came hurrying up to me,

'Your lion's half out,' she cried before making a very quick exit out of the zoo.

Still not really convinced I thought I'd better retrace my steps and take a look. To my horror the male had pulled a section of the wire fencing out of the ground and had managed to get his head and front paws almost through. Luckily, being a rather splendid male with an impressive mane to match his superiority, it had caught up in the wire, stopping him from going any further... Or so I thought.

A young keeper, Julie, who hadn't worked with us for very long, happened to be passing by.

'Julie, grab a bale of straw from the nearest animal house,' I shouted, while trying not to alert the public there was anything untoward happening.

With no time to spare I plugged the gap with the bale of straw, the lion even more intent on escaping. He was so close I could almost taste his breath, his head shaking from side to side, a guttural sound coming from deep within his body, wild eyes staring straight into my soul, his determination to get to me beyond doubt.

With the lion's huge paws sending the straw flying in all directions the bale was getting smaller and smaller. My back firmly pressed against the public barrier, both feet pressed onto the ever-disappearing bale, it being the only thing between me and a ferociously angry lion.

Thinking this isn't going to end well and with the scene resembling something out of a cartoon, I saw out of the corner of my eye an empty wire rubbish bin. Shouting to Julie to bring it over I forced it firmly into the gap.

By then the public had fled the scene and with the situation a little more under control I asked Julie to run to the curator's office to get some help.

Back then we didn't have radios for communication, just a referee's whistle for emergencies, but to blow it may have drawn the attention of any remaining public which I was trying hard to avoid.

After what seemed like a lifetime and with the lion ferociously attacking the metal bin, I was relieved to hear the sound of the Land Rover, with Peter, the curator on board.

A plan of action was soon put in place. With Julie dispatched inside the lion house working the internal slide I ran alongside the fencing towards the house closely followed by the lion, now free of the wire but still determined to get at me.

It worked and with the lion safely in the house, the slide securely in place my breathing began to return to normal.

'*We will meet up after lunch, Geoff,*' were Peters words as I headed off.

I got home to be greeted by Sandra saying, '*You're late today, I nearly gave up, lunch is probably cold by now.*'

With my legs starting to wobble the realisation of what had happened suddenly hit me, and after relaying, what could have been my last few moments on this earth, a little more sympathy was forthcoming.

After a quick, *cold*, lunch, I headed back to meet up with the curator to survey the scene.

It appeared that a two-foot stretch of wire mesh had somehow loosened at the bottom giving the lion leverage to pull it away.

Our director found me and thanked me for bravely stopping, what could have been a major incident. Not brave at all. When faced with a situation like that you do whatever needs doing, not to forget Julie who, being a fairly new keeper, kept her head in what was, for her, a baptism of fire.

Beautiful as the lions were, I admit to being a little relieved when a separate Carnivore section was created, and they were no longer under my care.

Sometimes, in the early hours of the morning I am sure I could still hear: '*Geoff, Geoff, Geoff.*'

Horses and Others

'*PULL ITS BLOODY HEAD UP,*' THE WOMAN BELLOWED. With her round face and rugged complexion, she appeared a force not to be argued with.

'I am trying,' I replied, and with a final heave the head went up and off we trotted.

Earlier that day, thinking, rather foolishly, it might be a fun day out to try a pony walk through the New Forest, I took the train to Hampshire, finally arriving at the equine stables where a rather beautiful, but exceptionally large horse awaited me. Mmm, not a pony as I thought.

She appeared placid enough, so trying to show more confidence than I felt I attempted to put my foot in the stirrup and climb up onto her back. After the third, very ungainly attempt I was finally in the saddle.

Listening very carefully to the instructions, I tried my hardest to pull her head up, however, she had other ideas, mainly to finish the grass she was so intent on eating.

Thinking I'd best take it easy as it seemed an awful long

way down from where I was sat, I started to relax and let the horse take the lead.

With the horse ambling along on a much familiar route through the forest my mind was on the beauty of the trees, their leaves glistened in the dappled sunlight, I was amazed at how much more could be seen from that height.

Not paying attention to what was in front of me I failed to notice the overhanging branch directly in my path; until… with an almighty thud it hit me squarely on the chin.

With a bleeding lip, bruised bum, and even worse injury to my pride I managed somehow to hold on to the reins while I spiralled downwards. Sitting firmly on the ground, embarrassment overcoming any pain I might have had from my injuries, I thought my instructor would be impressed that I had prevented the horse from galloping away without me. I was dismayed to hear her bellow the words, '*Get back on and pay attention!*'

Doing as I was told we continued our journey back at a much slower pace until, to my utter relief, the stables came into view.

That was my first and last attempt at horse riding. Though beautiful as they are, that day was the start of my love–hate relationship with equines.

Twelve years on and now at Marwell working with larger animals, I was dismayed to find equines featured as part of my section and my daily encounter with two Queen Victoria cream ponies did not fill me with any enthusiasm.

Regular grooming and hoof checks were a constant battle. The ponies I'm sure picked up on my hesitancy, strained their necks, and attempted to bite me at every given opportunity.

To make matters worse the children's zoo housed two donkeys. Now I have never been a big fan of donkeys in any shape or form, and although I despise the way they are treated in some countries, not forgetting the hours spent in the hot sun giving seaside rides to endless excited children here in England, it did not change my indifference to them as a species which was certainly cemented by my next encounter.

When the director says, *'Geoff have you got a minute?'* you start to worry.

'Have you heard of the Poitou donkey?'

Just hearing the word 'donkey' put me on edge.

'No, never heard of it,' was my apprehensive reply.

An overexcited Mr Knowles went on to explain the importance of this large, shaggy donkey originating from France. An important species in the equine world.

Oh, so, lucky me, Marwell would be looking after one for a while, and it was to be on my section.

Back home that evening, glass of wine in hand, I began my research, only a donkey, albeit a rather large one, I thought, you've handled worse, what could possibly go wrong?

Over the next few days an area was set aside for this very important donkey. A stable fit for a king, ready and waiting. And then, Theodore arrived. Tall, hairy, twice the size of any donkey I had ever seen, and oh, what big ears.

'What a handsome boy,' said Mr Knowles, gazing in awe at the sheer magnitude of this vast creature. *'And how docile.'*

Leaving Theodore to settle in overnight it was with a little trepidation that I approached his stable the following morning.

Slowly opening the door, talking quietly to reassure him, and with him walking calmly out I thought that maybe I should get to know him better, you never know I might even get to like him. Without any warning those huge ears went back, eyes rolling, mouth open showing a set of large menacing teeth and with unholy noise he came at me with such pace that the only way out was over the fence. With my heart thumping, a primal fear coursing through my veins I reached the fence and managed to jump over it, with seconds to spare before Theodore caught up with me.

Landing with a thud, legs and arms outstretched, my heart still racing, I glanced back to find Theodore grazing contentedly as if nothing had happened. Maybe we wouldn't become friends after all.

The only day the zoo closed was on Christmas Day itself. As I lived on site, I thought it only fair to give my keepers time off to spend with their families.

My Christmas Day consisted of a couple of hours in the morning spent feeding and cleaning, then home until the afternoon when I would go back to feed and settle the animals for the night.

Christmas morning and all was going well, just Theodore to let out and feed and I would be back home to watch the children open their presents. Feeling in a festive mood I quietly talked to him, letting him know what a good boy he really was. Thinking maybe I was getting somewhere with him I was little prepared for... Huge ears back, eyes rolling, teeth snarling, he again ran at me. With no time to get to the gate it was yet another leap over the fence before he hit it with such force, I thought it would buckle under his weight.

Finding myself, yet again, spread-eagled on the ground my first thought was at least I hadn't been killed on Christmas morning.

Knowing we would never really bond and only going in to see to him when necessary, I was rather pleased to be told he was going away for a while to be halter trained.

No chance: was my immediate thought when he was collected by a lady much smaller than him and me. Waving him goodbye I was convinced that I would soon hear of the poor lady's demise after being trampled by an oversize donkey.

As the day of Theodore's return got closer my feelings of unease came flooding back. I stood in disbelief the day he was brought back. The very same lady, alive and well, leading him quietly out of the horse box on a halter, just as if butter wouldn't melt until... any attempt on my part to go in with him.

So continued my love hate relationship with anything equine.

Holly the Hippo

WITH AN INCREASE IN VISITOR NUMBERS, FUNDS being available, and a growing awareness regarding animal welfare, plans were made for the building of new animal housing throughout the zoo, designed to meet the needs of specific species.

A purpose-built, semi-aquatic mammal house, to be located on the South Road, was part of the plan to house our pair of Brazilian Tapirs, plus two exciting new species, Pygmy Hippos and Malayan Tapirs.

The building was soon completed and with the added bonus of a mess room for the keepers; it was time for our Brazilian Tapirs to be moved into their new home.

Being peaceful animals, the move to new quarters went smoothly and in no time at all, they had settled into their new surroundings.

With the arrangements for the arrival of our first Malayan Tapir well underway the focus shifted to the collection of a female Pygmy Hippo, currently then residing at Edinburgh Zoo.

At 4am on a dark, cold, December morning I left the warmth of the cottage, making my way through the frozen field, frost crunching under my feet, the branches of the trees were dark and menacing in the pale moonlight.

Meeting up with Peter (curator), we set off for the long journey to Edinburgh. Cramped in an old Land Rover, the smell of diesel perpetrated my senses, I prepared myself for an awfully long and uncomfortable journey along endless motorways.

Feeling every back-breaking bump in the road, I wondered if I would ever walk again.

We finally arrived at our pre-booked B&B, a simple guest house with a warm welcome. Comfy beds guaranteed a much-needed night's sleep.

The following morning a hearty Scottish breakfast awaited us. No black pudding for me, thank you.

Arriving at Edinburgh Zoo we were met by the curator and given a short tour before collecting our new Hippo, who had been named Holly by her keepers.

With Holly safely crated in the back of the Land Rover we began our long journey home.

Along the same stretch of motorways, this time heading south. Travelling at a much slower speed, mindful of our extra passenger in the back, but despite this, still feeling every back-breaking bump in the road.

As day turned into night, we arrived back at Marwell and settled Holly into the holding pen for the reminder of the night, before making our way home. Never has the sight of our cottage looked so welcoming.

Pygmy hippos are relatively smaller than their closely related common hippo, measuring around 70 cm in height, and weighing up to 275 kg. With sharp teeth and large canines, they are known for their aggression. Holly was no exception. Despite their size they are remarkably agile, being able to move very quickly, which I later found to my dismay.

Just as any other day the morning cleaning routine in the semi-aquatic house began when I noticed Holly had caught her bottom canine teeth in the mesh surrounding the edge of the pool. Being unable to close her mouth and with saliva building up I knew I had to act fast. With broom in hand, I began trying to push her jaw downwards in order to free the teeth, not an easy task with an irate hippo. Despite some difficulty I finally succeeded, although it was clear my rescue actions were not appreciated.

Get out quick, was my next thought, with my only choice being to quickly climb on the edge surrounding the pool.

Just when I thought I was safe Holly managed to grab the buckle on my wellington boot and, between her force and my slight athleticism, ripped it clean off.

To decorate the edge of the pool, tubs containing large banana plants had been strategically placed, instinctually I grabbed the nearest stem. Breathing a sigh of relief, thinking I was safe, it had not occurred to me the planters were on wheels.

As if on roller skates with ever-increasing speed I travelled closer and closer to the edge of the pool, a truly angry Hippo, mouth wide open, snapping at my legs, determined to do some serious damage. The plant suddenly and without warning toppled over into the pool and disappeared into several feet of murky water.

Somehow with legs dangling I managed to grab onto the

ledge, seconds away from disaster, before hauling myself to safety.

With heart rate slowly getting back to normal and Holly none the worse for our exploits I let her out into the paddock, shutting the gate firmly behind her.

Then began the great clean-up operation. With the banana plant now firmly seated on the bottom of the pool I realised I would need some help and to avoid any embarrassment I stuck to the story it had just *toppled over and fallen in.*

With a rescue operation in full swing and after a quick hose down, it looked as good as new. Without wanting any further confrontation, I decided NOT to confess to Sue (our plant lady).

Sue, if you are reading this, I apologise now.

The Royal Visit

A s with the majority of new exhibits at Marwell there was to be an official opening of the Semi Aquatic House.

The day duly arrived with HRH Duchess of Kent in attendance.

My daughter Angela presented her with a bouquet and a well-practised curtsy.

As always, the press had been invited and with a large crowd gathered, I was asked if they could get a photograph of HRH petting one of the animals.

With my skating experience still uppermost in my mind I thought maybe the Tapirs would be the most suitable due to their calm nature.

Following a tour of the section I asked HRH if she would like to meet the Tapirs up close to which she willingly agreed.

Knowing these animals very well I was aware that the male Tapir's initial greeting was to scent mark his surroundings by squirting urine.

With the female quietly resting it was the male who ambled over to lie down in front of the Duchess who stroked him amid the rush of clicking cameras, job well done.

As the press started to leave the building the Duchess lingered asking more questions about the Tapirs. Noticing the male starting to stand up I quickly moved between him and the Duchess when I was horrified to feel a rather warm wetness on the back of my leg. Knowing I had been scented, it was a feeling of relief he had chosen me and not her. I did wonder if she had noticed.

Our New Arrival

'MUM, SHAAN'S PULLED THE CURTAINS DOWN AGAIN,' shouted Aron.

'Dad, Shaan's taken an apple from the fruit bowl, and she is eating it!' called out Angie.

Trying to restore order amongst the ever-increasing chaos within our family home I grabbed Shaan and placed her on the rope climbing frame I had built under the dining room table.

Dear reader, before you contact the NSPCC please let me explain.

It was after work on a balmy spring evening that my family saw me walking up the path to the cottage with a cardboard box cradled in my arms. I can still hear my wife Sandra groaning with anticipation as to what was hidden within and how many sleepless nights it entailed.

It wasn't uncommon in the early days to hand rear rejected animals, usually it was an antelope, even the occasional cat, but this was a little different.

Our Indonesian Siamang Gibbon, 'Dara' had never in the past been a particularly good mother and immediately after giving birth this time, she rejected this little female. Previously the decision had been made that should this happen we would give the baby a chance and attempt to hand rear it. As head keeper I felt it was my duty to volunteer for the task.

With the children gathered round I opened the box to unveil this little, and to be honest, not very attractive baby primate.

Seeing her tucked up with a warm hot water bottle and wrapped in a foil blanket the female contingency of the family fell in love with her straight away. The boys, I think, felt the same but being boys, it wasn't the done thing to show it.

The basic care of a new-born primate is similar to that of a human baby; thank goodness we had some experience of that to fall back on.

Our first thought was where to obtain milk and after much deliberation we opted for new-born baby milk, as gibbon milk wasn't readily available in the supermarket. For hygiene purposes our next task was to find the tiniest nappies available.

Our first port of call was the maternity department at Winchester hospital where we asked to be put through to the premature baby unit.

Despite disbelief and threats of transferring our call to the psychiatric department the staff were very helpful and agreed to our request for a box of nappies.

Milk and nappies sorted. Our next task was finding something suitable for her to sleep in, a little tricky as normally she would be clinging to her mum's chest for heat. A modified box with blankets, hot water bottle and one of Angela's cuddly toys did the trick until we borrowed a carry cot from a very bemused friend.

The regime of two-hourly feeding and nappy changing was undertaken by all the family, with the children readily taking turns, except during the night when this fell to Sandra as, having raised three children, she had the most experience with night feeds.

By this time and after much discussion (arguments) between the children the name Shaan was decided upon, for no particular reason, they just liked the name.

As the weeks went on Shaan grew stronger with her care becoming part of family life. With the children having a very long waiting list of school friends wanting to come to tea and play with Shaan there was never a dull moment; the sound of children's voices with Shaan trying to mimic them, to any outsider would be an unusual, if not interesting mix, but very much the norm in our household.

Despite the situation, we were very aware of our responsibility of not humanising her, an extremely difficult balancing act. Gibbons, being arboreal, have long powerful arms and need to have that muscle built up for later life. I spent a lot of time encouraging her to grab my thumbs and swing a little, as she would in a primate group in order to start this happening. Even at this young age her grip was amazing.

Our local newspaper got to hear about Shaan and sent a reporter and photographer to meet her and our family. Publicity is often welcomed by zoos to profile events and to create interest in the important conservation work carried out, mostly behind the scenes. A now very cute baby primate living in a family home would make an interesting story and we managed to get the message of conservation and education across as well as the ahhh factor.

My own personal opinion is that publicity is ok, as long as it does not demean the animal. Tasteful photo shoot over, and with respectful journalists on their way, it was back to our version of normality, whatever that might be.

As Shaan's development continued we had to devise various methods of improving her strength and skills; she was after all a tree swinging gibbon. An old indoor clothes rack with lengths of first aid bandages wrapped around it to make several levels became a makeshift climbing frame, where she could swing as if among the trees. She took to it straight away her natural instinct and ability proving how easy it was for her to manoeuvre around. It was so satisfying to see her safely using my invention to build up her muscles.

Clothes rack conquered we progressed to the dining room table wrapping more bandages and small ropes around the legs which she appeared to find a lot more challenging and great fun.

With growing confidence Shaan's next adventure was to tackle the fruit and vegetable rack where she took great delight in helping herself to whatever was on hand. Rather like a naughty child she would look to see if anyone were watching her exploits and if they were, she would look you in the eye as her hand reached towards the chosen fruit.

As time went on, although she responded to all the attention from the family, it was me she clung to and just like a child would hold her rather long arms out to be picked up.

A trip into the garden was a great learning curve for us both and putting her on small tree branches was the ultimate test in her development. It was during this time we heard her make her first Gibbon sound, a series of 'Hoo' noises which gradually got louder as her throat sac inflated forcing out the sound. The excitement we felt, just like when a baby says its first words, was short-lived. Her calls became louder and longer as time went on, reverberating around the cottage and far into the garden.

There were times when Sandra had other things to do apart from Gibbon sitting which meant I had to take Shaan to work with me. Not an easy feat cleaning up rhino poo with a gibbon strapped to your chest. The journey to work was easy, walking through the bridleway stopping every now and then to allow Shaan to swing from a low tree branch pointing out the various wildlife accompanying us on our journey.

Walking home from work was a different matter altogether. My last job of the day was to check all the animals on my section, which meant walking home through the zoo. With the public still milling around a keeper walking along with a young gibbon attached was unusual to say the least. As much as I was always happy to stop and talk to the public the fact it would take me twice as long to get home became a bit wearing, so much so that I changed my evening routine and walked back home through the bridleway.

As time went on with Shaan growing bigger and stronger and very much louder, she thought nothing of joining in the dawn chorus regardless of what time in the morning. As well as waking up our household I'm sure the villagers 3.5 miles away wondered what on earth the noise was.

Shaan became quite a celebrity at the village school. With education in mind, I would often take her into the classroom, giving talks on wildlife and how important conservation was to ensure the survival of all wild animals. The children would make thank you cards for Shaan to take home with her, something we all appreciated.

A reminder to our curator that the young Gibbon in our care was approaching 8 months old and needed to be with her own kind was issued. After many discussions as to where she would be best suited and cared for, the decision was made to take her to Twycoss Zoo in Atherstone, Warwickshire as they specialised very successfully in primates.

The founder and director the late Molly Badham had a passion for primates and was instrumental in the care of the Brooke Bond tea chimps in the famous TV commercials in the 1960s.

The day of Shaan leaving home finally arrived and with the family saying their very tearful goodbyes Peter (curator) and I set off on the long journey to Warwickshire. With Shaan in a custom-made container but still able to see out, like a child on a long car journey she alternated between sleeping, fidgeting, and becoming very vocal.

Arriving at Twycross we were greeted by Molly and her primate keeper and taken to a building where Shaan would spend a period of time getting used to new surroundings and people.

I have to be totally honest that taking her out of the container and leaving her was very difficult but with a lump in my throat it had to be done. I knew she would be in exceptional hands.

After some lunch and a tour of the zoo we headed back to where a much quieter home awaited me.

After a settling in period of about a year we decided it was time to visit Shaan in her new home which she now shared with a hand-reared male of roughly the same age.

'Do you want to go in with her?' I was asked. Not needing any encouragement, I readily agreed and ventured in.

To my delight Shaan appeared to recognise me; she came straight over wanting to be picked up and played with the cord on my sweatshirt just like when she was a baby. Time just rolled back, and I stood transfixed, memories of the tiny baby wrapped in a foil blanket, going through my mind, until... I noticed the male Gibbon becoming more and more agitated and thinking he would soon start to show his dominance I decided it was time to make a quick exit.

Speaking to the Gibbon keepers was quite an eye opener as I was informed that on more than one occasion while taking Shaan for her daily walk around the zoo she took it upon herself to invade the zoo restaurant. Darting under the tables she caused mayhem, swinging amongst the bemused diners' legs, foraging into their handbags for tasty morsels. Chaos reigned, until her keepers brought her back under control.

'It's obviously her upbringing,' I was told, and with a smile I thought about our dining room table with its rope and bandaging. Maybe they were right.

In most zoos these days hand rearing is not encouraged unless really necessary. The negative impact on human imprinting has been well documented in many animal species and as time has progressed, where possible, other less damaging techniques have been developed to assist with conservation and to ensure the security of healthy, stable populations of countless species.

Sadly, Shaan has since passed away but she has left a legacy of fond memories, sleepless nights, and an amazing experience for all the family who supported me and worked so hard to ensure her a secure and safe start in life.

Fierce Creatures

A T THE START OF A NORMAL WORKING DAY A MESSAGE
was sent to all staff to attend a meeting. With us
all congregating in the great hall Mr Knowles made the
announcement that a film unit would be moving into the
zoo for three days filming their new production, *Fierce
Creatures*, a sequel to the 1980s film *A Fish Called Wanda*.
For the three days Marwell Zoo would become Marwood
Zoo.

Much to my excitement we soon discovered that an all-
star cast was to be headed by my personal favourite actor,
John Cleese.

More information on the actors was forthcoming, with
such stars as Jamie Lee Curtis, Kevin Kline, Ronnie Corbett,
and Derek Griffiths, with Michael Palin and Robert Lindsay,
in the starring roles.

With a buzz of excitement going around the zoo, and
with the thought of a change to their daily routine, a renewed
sense of energy emerged among the keepers.

The theme of the film was of an American multi-millionaire who had bought a zoo in England but with attendances falling the zoo's director, played by John Cleese, decided that to save the zoo from closure only fierce animals would be housed, hence the name *Fierce Creatures*.

The fictional keepers planned to falsely claim that all the animals were fierce, thus saving the zoo and their livelihoods.

Marwell keepers, including me, would be involved as non-speaking extras and to help and advise on any aspect of the animals.

With drum roll and lights blazing, at last the time came for my acting debut, albeit with trepidation as I thought back to my disastrous television appearance with the bees.

Take one and the filming began. A Marwood keeper (actor) with a chair for protection pretending to fend off a slightly bewildered South American Coati, the aim to convince the zoo director it was an extremely dangerous animal. My role in the scene, alongside another keeper David, was to stand in the background with two camels. Whacka, named for his ability to give a sharp whack to anyone standing in his way and Tabitha, a more reserved lady. Both camels were trained to give rides, so were familiar with being led and once in position portrayed their role convincingly.

A few takes and performance over we made our way back to the camel house.

Uphill no problem, downhill another matter.

Camel racing, being a popular sport in some countries, but not, I must add, in the hilly terrain at Marwell... BUT! the camels thought differently.

With each Camel weighing up to 1000kg and capable of running at 30mph, rather than leading them, we found ourselves hanging on gathering speed at an alarming rate, downhill, past the Hall on the right, fast approaching the camel's quarters, the scenery around us flashing quickly by until at last we reached the bottom of the hill where skidded to a halt, hoping we hadn't been seen, we brushed ourselves down before continuing on as if nothing untoward had happened.

Another scene and my next assignment involved our three White Rhinos. Compared to the camel fiasco this is going to be easy, or so I thought.

With the film crew ready my role was to take the Rhinos to an area in the background but to keep them in shot, while a complicated piece of filming was taking place.

Like us humans, animals usually follow a well-rehearsed night-time routine. At the same time, every evening you would find the rhinos waiting at the entrance to their house for their feed before being settled into their night quarters. Without this routine, well, let's just say things can get a little unsettled.

With filming taking longer than we all anticipated and with an hour past their bedtime the Rhinos decided to give up and go and sulk in the farthest corner of the paddock. The film crew were becoming increasingly worried that we would be unable to persuade the Rhinos to come back on set. Easy I thought, no need to panic, I knew my Rhinos.

I jumped into the paddock, amid the look of horror on the gathering crew's faces. (*Was this idiot really going in with three heavyweight Rhinos!*)

My first London Zoo uniform

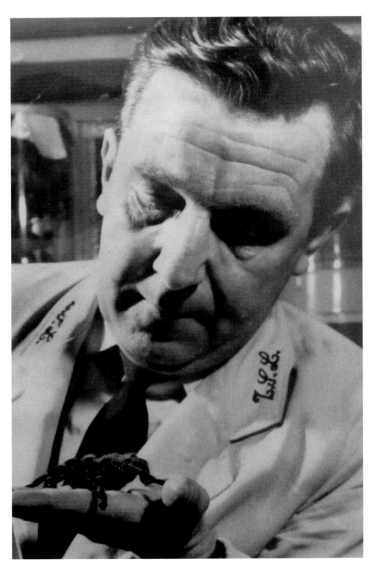

My London Zoo head keeper, Bob Humphries. The man who taught me so much

Shaan, our hand-reared Gibbon at two hours old

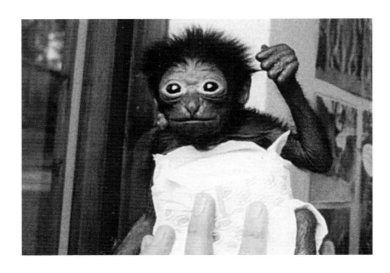

She will grow into that nappy!

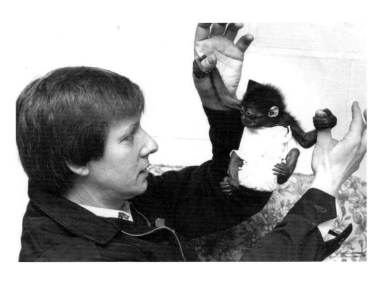

Shaan's daily exercise routine

Me and Shaan on our way to work

My daughter Angie bottle feeding a Giraffe

Marwell's first Pygmy Hippo baby enjoying a summer shower

Sula and Bhasela

Bhasela at three days old

Meet and greet with Royalty

Princess Royal opening Penguin World at Marwell

As I said I knew my animals and started calling them over. Rhino's eyesight is pretty poor, but they knew the sound of my voice and one by one started ambling over to me. The initial horror of the crew turned to astonishment and with much praise, I grudgingly admitted there had been no risk involved; with filming complete, I was able to settle the Rhinos down for the night.

The very next morning John Cleese found me in with the Rhinos where he thanked me for the previous evening's achievement.

To his genuine delight I managed to persuade our beautiful female, Sula, to come over for him to stroke.

He agreed that you couldn't put a price on what was to me, a daily privilege.

Discussing the breeding of these beautiful animals I described to him, in great detail, about a particular mating I had observed that hadn't quite gone to plan.

To my delight he found my antidotes very funny.

My claim to fame. I have made the great and brilliant comedian John Cleese laugh.

Down Under

'GEOFF, DO YOU WANT TO GO TO AUSTRALIA?' ASKED Peter our assistant curator.

Without a second thought, my answer was a resounding yes.

Marwell was providing a quantity of animals for a zoo in Western Australia, which was owned by Lord McAlpine, a British businessman and politician.

Prior to the journey the animals would need a 30-day period of intensive quarantine.

My role was to look after the animals for the quarantine period and then accompany them, alongside Peter and two vets for their long journey to Australia.

Back home that evening, with the family all around me, I explained that I would going away for a few days.

'Can we come with you, Dad?' asked the children.

I explained that Australia was a long way away, that I had to go on an aeroplane and that I needed them to stay behind to help look after the animals.

Dad going away soon forgotten, the children started to discuss (argue) who was going to look after what, which of them would have the most important job and more importantly, would they earn extra pocket money.

'As I'm the eldest I should be in charge,' said Aron.

This was met with a collective shout from the other children, no way was that going to happen!

The bickering continued until... Sandra who had been unusually quiet up to that point, suggested that they drew up a rota between them. They readily agreed and with paper and pencils collected, the children began the task.

'As I'm the eldest I should do the writing,' said Aron. The bickering continued.

Later in the evening, shedding a few tears, Sandra admitted to feeling sad that I was going away but realised what an amazing opportunity it was for me.

Quarantine regulations were, and still are, extremely strict. I was not allowed any contact with any other livestock including my own milking goat, in case of any cross infection. Luckily, a neighbouring farmer came to our rescue and agreed to have our goats for the set period of my absence.

And it began, I was officially assigned off section until quarantine had been completed.

Four unused areas within the zoo were set aside to house the chosen animals whilst they were in quarantine. All were steam cleaned, kitted out with all the necessary cleaning utensils, plus enough food, hay, and straw to last the 30 days.

With disinfectant footbaths, wellies, and a very fetching blue zip-up suits in place we were at last ready. This was a major task.

First to be moved were seven Przewalski's horses, followed by three Grevy Zebras, two Congo Buffalo, five Sitatunga, four Nyala, one Llama, one Kudu and three Gemsbok.

Not a Partridge in a pear tree in sight!

Blood samples had to be taken, TB tests plus all the necessary inoculations complete. Last but not least, for the final fourteen days a daily inspection by a Ministry vet was a statuory requirement.

It proved to be an interesting period, both from a specific husbandry point of view and providing a chance for me to spend as much time as possible to win the trust of the animals during their long journey ahead.

All the crates had been carefully made, both for animal and aircraft design. Feeding hatches had to be included so as to eliminate the risk of an animal escaping when opening the slide. The last thing we wanted on a long-haul flight was wild animals running amok.

Once the animals were safely in the crates and loaded onto the lorry, we began the journey to Stanstead Airport.

Following behind the convoy of lorries making their way slowly along the motorway I wondered what the other road users thought? How many of them, at the sight of the slow-moving procession of lorries, would have guessed the unusual precious cargo we carried? Zero probably.

As the journey continued, I began to realise the enormity of the task I was undertaking. Not only was I partly responsible for the safety and wellbeing of the animals, but I was also leaving my family to fend for themselves while I travelled to the other side of the world. So, it was with mixed feelings of sadness and excitement that I watched the animals being loaded onto the British Airways freight plane.

Before long it was our turn to board. Finding ourselves tightly squeezed in seats positioned as far back in the plane as possible and after a smooth take-off we were finally airborne.

I had never flown before and there I was flying halfway round the world. A true baptism of fire. I was feeling a little nervous to say the least, I was extremely grateful for the advice given by friends.

'*Don't look down. Make sure you get the only parachute,*' and the best of all from my very good friend Bill was, '*make sure you sit at the back as aeroplanes don't reverse into mountains.*'

A constant welfare check was made on all the individual animals. The first routine taking us nearly four hours. As dehydration could become a problem, we had to ensure the animals regularly took liquids, soaking hay in water as an extra precaution.

With the animal crates being secured at the front of the plane and with us at the back I was horrified to see a sea of bright yellow animal urine with a strangely distinct sweet, acidic smell, being swept towards us every time the plane ascended to new heights. With nowhere to run it was to my utter relief that I watched it disappear down a gully before it reached our feet.

The first stop on our journey was in Edmonton, Canada to refuel. Due to quarantine regulations we had to remain on board the aircraft. A single step on the tarmac would have been disastrous and further quarantine rules imposed.

Before taking off again the steward asked if there was a virgin on board, bit personal I thought, someone who had never flown, he added to my relief.

I reluctantly confessed and before I knew it, I was in the cockpit behind the captain ready for take-off.

Dozens of flight-checks later, we were off and up, flying over the Rocky Mountains, an experience never to be forgotten. Remembering the sound advice from Bill, that planes don't reverse into mountains. The nervousness gave way to the amazing experience.

Next stop Honolulu, a few paperwork problems to sort out, legs stretched and we were soon air bound again.

More feeding and watering continued, though the routine got quicker and easier with practice. It was good to see the animals, so far, had shown no signs of stress.

Our next stop was Auckland, New Zealand, where we were allowed off the plane onto the tarmac, to stretch our legs. What a good feeling that was.

At last, after a further nine hours in the air, our first stop in Australia, Adelaide, and the final destination for our Przewalski's horses. Next stop would be Perth, Western Australia, our final destination.

After the grand total of forty-eight hours in the air we finally arrived in Perth where we began unloading our precious cargo of animals. The rest of our journey was by road to Perth Zoo. A convoy of lorries took us and the animals, still safely in their crates, on the final twenty-minute journey.

On arrival we were greeted by a former member of Marwell staff, Joe Haddock, who now worked at Perth Zoo.

Unloading the animals was a fairly easy task but we had not considered there is no twilight in Western Australia. Without warning daylight disappeared and darkness fell so it was a race against time to get the task completed.

With the animals settled, it was our turn to be fed and watered, and then the tiredness overcame me. If I stopped moving, without a doubt, I knew I would fall asleep.

Peter and I made our way to our accommodation, an extremely comfortable colonial-style house. After a quick telephone call home, I bedded down for the night, realisation set in that I had been awake for forty-eight hours.

A new day dawned, and with plans to check that all the animals were well and settled in their new quarters, we took the opportunity to look around Perth Zoo.

Feeling slightly jet lagged and walking with legs that had been sat down for far too long I gingerly made my way around the vast wilderness of Perth Zoo. Up and down hill until I reached yet another paddock created from part of the Australian outback. I was utterly impressed at the amount of space the animals had, noticing how well looked after they were and the cleanliness of everything. Oops, sorry, talking with my head keeper's hat on. There were clean containers filled to the brim with fresh water for the animals to drink from and plenty of shade for the animals to rest away from the blistering heat. For them it was almost like being in the wild.

The following day even more travel, this time on a local aircraft for the two-and-a-half-hour journey to Broome, a coastal town in the Kimberley region.

Flying low over this vast wasteland of red soil made me realise the enormity of this beautiful, almost prehistoric country. I had visions of dinosaurs roaming wild, millions upon millions of years ago. I was convinced, and still am, there must be areas that no human has ever set foot on.

On arrival we were taken first to our accommodation, another colonial-style house with large rooms and the furniture in keeping with the period. All the windows were meshed at the top to prevent mosquitoes and sand flies entering. Despite my interest and liking of insects, this was something I was incredibly pleased about.

We were then taken to the zoo to be given a tour around by Trevor, the zoo curator.

The final destination for our animals to take up residence was large areas of natural bush, fenced off with some landscaping and man-made lakes, it made an ideal setting for our Sitatunga and Kudu alike.

Apart from my misgivings about basic husbandry in such large areas I was happy knowing our animals would have the freedom to roam, as if in the wild.

Our day ended with a full-on Australian barbie (BBQ) hosted at his home by Trevor and his family. An array of well-cooked meats was in abundance. Some easily recognised, some not. Did I really want to know what they were? I think not. With conversation going on around me, I sat gazing out over the bush. The midnight black of the sky awash with millions of stars, brighter and bigger than I had ever seen before. I was mesmerised by the sounds of insects cutting their way through the undergrowth, some I recognised, others new and alien to me.

As the night drew to a close and with the promise of a road trip the following day to see some of Australia's native wildlife, we bid our farewells and made our way back to our accommodation and another good night's sleep.

A new day, and true to his word Trevor arrived and we soon found ourselves aboard a Land Rover for the pleasant, if somewhat bumpy, ride to the Australian outback.

We saw masses of Wallabies, colourful Parrots, and Cockatoos with their spectacular red tails, and other small birds in vast numbers, Pelicans, and many species of Eagle. I was in awe of the diversity of wildlife and the wilderness of rugged landscape they inhabit in that wild and beautiful country.

It was all too soon time to say goodbye and make my way to the airport to catch the late afternoon flight back to England. Leaving Broome in temperatures of 33°C I arrived in Perth in the rain to catch the 3.20pm flight on a Boeing 747. A little different to the cargo plane we arrived in, this one had comfy seats and lots of them.

An eight-hour delay in Singapore added to the journey time and after what seemed like forever, I finally found myself back on home turf.

It was an amazing experience; I was proud to be an ambassador for Marwell sharing our knowledge and working practices with fellow keepers while at the same time learning how they managed their animals on such a vast scale was exacting but rewarding.

Pleased to be home even if a little jet lagged. Sandra and the children wanting to hear about my adventures. The children all talking at once to tell me theirs. How they had looked after the animals for me, what they had done at school and how many new camps they had built.

Trips away to foreign lands are all very good but the reality of family and work was what I really missed and wanted. Plus of course milking the goats.

Our Good Life

A HERD OF FEMALE PYGMY GOATS, ALWAYS POPULAR with the public, were housed in the children's zoo and with thoughts of a great display of agile goat kids in the spring we began actively searching for a breeding male.

Enter, Marjorie, a local goat breeder, no nonsense, down to earth lady with a wealth of knowledge and, more importantly, a male pygmy goat which she was happy to loan to us.

After meeting with Marjorie several times and introducing her to the family she asked if I would like to meet her herd of Saanen milking goats. How could I refuse such an offer?

Throughout the short journey to meet them, Marjorie described the benefits of goat's milk, no more buying cheese, or yoghurts and no more milk bills.

Arriving at Marjorie's small holding, which consisted of a few sheds in a fairly large field I was introduced to the goats, six in all, with white short coats and long straggly beards, all individually named.

Marjorie then took me into the goat sheds; in there hung the sweet smell of hay and goat that would stay on your skin and clothing long after you had left.

With the thought of fresh milk at just the cost of goat food I was becoming extremely interested indeed. I just had to convince Sandra.

Back home, with the family gathered around, I relayed all that Marjorie had said, adding that now we were *country folk* we should live the good life and try our hand at self-sufficiency.

I think my enthusiasm must have rubbed off and with everyone agreeing I contacted Marjorie to arrange a date to collect our first goat, named Tracey.

Adjoining our cottage was a large field, enclosed by the zoo's perimeter fence making it a secure area with good grass and plenty of shrubbery, an ideal outside area for the goat.

Next somewhere for her to live, and after purchasing wood and a door from the reclaim yard the building of the goat shed began. With much enthusiasm and help from Aron and Vince it was soon in place, with all its splendour, at the back of the garden.

Following advice on milking, given to us by Marjorie, plus a lot of research, we began purchasing the items needed, milking buckets, freezer bags, udder cleaning wipes and a metal tether and chain.

Tracey duly arrived, a large girl, pure white with heavy udders and an impressive long white beard.

Leaving her to settle in her new home I prepared myself for the first milking.

Mindful of the advice to be gentle, due to my rather large hands. I was very relieved to have milked out four pints while Tracey contentedly ate from her food bucket.

Back indoors as the light began to fade, I began dreaming of a self-sufficient lifestyle, like a farmer tending his flock I pondered what our next venture would be.

'*Now we've got a goat can we have chickens?*' the children asked.

'That's a great idea,' was my immediate reply, with just a tiny thought in the back of my mind as to how we were going to house them.

Looking through a poultry magazine I was impressed by one of the chicken arks, but as money was tight, I decided I would make my own.

With truly little knowledge of building anything bigger than a bird box, but, I add, full of enthusiasm I thought, what could possibly go wrong?

Wood and wire purchased and with the weather outside blowing a gale it seemed the most sensible thing to do was to begin building it indoors. With the dining room cleared work commenced.

After a few choice words and numerous cups of tea I had proudly finished the framework, even adding a hinged door on the inside area.

With the sun at last shining, I thought it would be safer to staple the wire to the frame outside.

Now reading this you may be ahead of me, but have you ever tried to get an 8ft /× 4ft × 3 ft high chicken ark through a three-foot-wide door!!

The family were, of course, very supportive, and after

wiping away tears of laughter gave me various words of wisdom on what to do next.

After a little dismantling and the removal of the fairly large dining room window, we managed to manoeuvre the newly built coop outside.

With Sandra and the boys shaking their heads in disbelief I had the unenviable task of rebuilding the ark and putting the dining room window back in its rightful place. Lesson learnt the hard way, but the family had rallied together as we always did, to solve our problems.

Oh, how we laughed.

The next step was to position the said chicken ark in its final resting place.

With help from Aron and Vince, we carefully manoeuvred it through the garden and into the field, trying to avoid the abundance of stinging nettles, growing nicely, ready to be turned into wine. (Oh yes, I was going full out on this self-sufficiency stuff!)

The three of us walking up and down the field carrying a very heavy ark while struggling to find the perfect position was a sight to behold.

Our next job was to purchase the chickens. A well-known egg production company had a unit based nearby, which housed battery hens. At the end of their short intense laying season the hens were sold for re-homing.

With the thought of newly laid free-range eggs, we purchased twelve hens, most of which were in a deeply sorry state with few feathers and beaks that had been cut to stop them pecking each other. A lot of TLC would be needed over the next few weeks.

Once home we introduced our girls to their new ark, where they huddled together in one corner, fearful of so much freedom. Leaving them warm and safe with plenty of food and water we retreated back to the cottage for the night.

The next morning saw us all congregating outside the ark, with some trepidation as to what we might find.

Door open one by one our girls ventured outside instinctively scratching at the unfamiliar grass and stretching their wings. After several weeks, their feathers had grown back, they looked the picture of health and were laying the most beautiful brown free-range eggs. Time to rescue more hens.

Within no time at all with another ark purchased this time (I couldn't go through the fiasco of building one again), we had thirty hens and a most handsome grey Maran cockerel, named Sampson, to keep his girls in order. He certainly had his work cut out.

With everything running smoothly both in the home and the small holding, I thought it was time for Sandra and me to have an overnight break on our own. With Sandra's mum readily agreeing to look after the children and with a good friend milking the goat twice-a-day we were at last ready for our first time ever, away without the children.

Staying in a comfy B&B in the New Forest we had an enjoyable two days exploring the area but not, I might add, not going anywhere near the wild ponies that roam freely there!

Returning home well rested we were greeted by the sight of an extremely tired-looking mother-in-law.

'Everything was fine,' she said, 'except… it took me a good hour to get the chickens back into the ark before it got dark.'

Explaining that the chickens knew their routine and return home on their own before nightfall without being chased around the field was maybe something I should have said before we left.

Spring arrived and with my thoughts turned to more animals for our small holding I approached the subject of a couple of new-born orphaned lambs, to hand rear as meat for our freezer. Four extremely excited children agreed at once but had to be reminded of the lamb's destiny, and the fact it was not a good idea to give them names. Sandra took a little persuading as she thought of the two-hourly feeds required.

Good quality sheep fencing was purchased along with sturdy posts and in no time at all a fair-sized area materialised with a roofed shelter that even I was proud of.

Soon after we found ourselves once again visiting the local farm to purchase two very noisy, lively two-day old lambs.

Driving home with the children taking turns in holding the lambs which were by then quite sleepy and well behaved disaster struck in the way of a punctured tyre.

And of course, as always when this happens, it was raining.

Changing a tyre in the rain, down a narrow country lane, with four children, and two lambs which had by then woken up and were bleating loudly as new-borns do, was not my idea of fun.

Sandra thought otherwise and instigated a sing-song of 'Old McDonald Had A Farm'. With the children singing and the lambs bleating, the poor unsuspecting driver who stopped to help made a hasty retreat back to his vehicle.

Home at last. Using our own goat's milk, the two-hourly bottle-feeding regimes began, and with the whole family taking turns, it promised to be an easy task.

Now you may recall I said it's better not to name them as their stay was not going to be an awfully long one and as always, my word was law.

With Duncan and James as they had been named, the lambs were settled in well. The boys decided, when it was their turn to feed them, they would do it upstairs in their bedroom. Before long, the noise of two lads and two half grown sheep racing up and down stairs became the norm in the Read household.

With weaning coming to an end and their growth rate increasing the outside world beckoned and the sheep pen was duly opened. With a plentiful supply of grass, good feed, and space to roam they appeared settled in their outside quarters.

Now I know sheep are not supposed to be bright, but Duncan was special!

Hearing him bleating one morning we checked to discover he had his head stuck through the *so-called* sheep mesh.

With no harm done we managed to push his head back through and carried on with our chores. After 10 minutes the same noise with the same result, after another 15 minutes yes you guessed it. He was as I said '*special*'.

Occasionally they would both jump the fence and run straight into the cottage, through the dining room, into the lounge and straight upstairs until they reached the boys' bedroom. Another sight to behold was the two boys and myself carrying two very heavy, fully grown sheep back down the stairs.

When the time came for them to leave us, we knew we had given them a good life, albeit a short one.

What started with one milking goat turned into a menagerie of self-sufficiency.

One goat became three; thirty chickens and Samson continued to roam free giving us an abundance of eggs for ourselves and to sell or barter for other things.

With enough space in the field Sandra thought it would be nice to have our own honey and with the London Zoo TV disaster of smoking the bees still firmly in my mind it took some persuasion before I finally agreed to the purchase of two hives of fully established bees.

Bee husbandry is a mix of common sense with attention to detail; checking every twelve days for developing queen cells is a priority, also keeping stock of the amount of honey produced and tallying enough feed for the colony especially during winter months.

All was going well and with a full harvest of honey disaster struck...

Tracey, our goat, somehow pulled her tether out of the ground and made her way around the field happily munching on the grass until her loose tether got caught up at the bottom of the hive and eventually, she accidentally pulled it over.

With incredibly angry bees swarming out of the hive, a panicking goat and a sense of déjà vu, I did my best to reinstate order. With the goat settled, the bees back in the hive protecting their queen I questioned my role as a beekeeper.

Sadly, the hive never fully recovered and with the bees swarming from one hive and the other being hit by the parasitic Varroa mite it was one of our less successful ventures. I just have to admit bees are not my forte!

Undeterred our good life continued. Geese was the next plan.

'Goose at Christmas, Bob Cratchit?'

A pair of geese was duly acquired, two magnificent creatures with an attitude.

Being exceptionally good guard geese, they even attacked Sandra when she attempted to hang out the washing. Fearing for the children we made a difficult decision and found them a new home on a local farm.

'Free-range turkeys,' we thought, *'a Christmas treat.'*

Research completed, two grown-on turkey poults were purchased which duly arrived. They grew quite quickly, so, we decided to let them roam in the field. Free-range turkeys, what a treat. This worked very well; the turkeys never wandered away and always came running, as only turkeys can run, for food.

The day before Christmas Eve arrived, the birds were humanly slaughtered and with the thought of a nice plump free-range turkey for Christmas dinner the plucking of feathers began... With enough feathers to fill a double eiderdown, the flesh EVENTUALLY appeared the size of a pigeon. Although free ranging was great for the welfare of the birds, they had run off all their fat, so what should have been a nice Christmas centrepiece turned out to be a teatime snack.

With Christmas a distant memory, and winter turning into spring, I no longer had to fumble my way to the goat shed in the dark for the morning milking.

'Not sure what's wrong with Tracey today, she's off her food and seems incredibly quiet,' I said. 'Best keep our eye on her.'

Letting Rosie and Twinkle, our other two goats, out into the field I decided to leave Tracey in to recover from whatever ailment she appeared to have.

Over the next week or so Tracey seemed a bit better but still wasn't her usual self, and although eating she had lost some of her usual sparkle and a lot of weight.

Early one morning when entering the goat shed, I found Tracey lying on her side.

'Come on, old girl, up you get,' I said as Tracey tried to stand, but could only manage to lift her head, her eyes darting from side to side, she was obviously in pain.

Gently rubbing my hand over her abdomen, I felt a large bulge inside, and from that moment, knew there could be only one outcome. Contacting the zoo vet was one of the hardest things I have had to do, and as the children came in one by one to say their goodbyes the vet arrived.

Confirming my diagnosis which turned out to be a cancerous mass we agreed the kindest thing would be to gently send her to sleep.

I slowly knelt down by her side as the needle was inserted. She didn't move but quietly and peacefully her breathing stopped. As her eyes glassed over, I knew we had done the right thing by her and that she would no longer feel any pain.

That evening we all shed a few tears, tinged with laughter, at the many antics Tracey had got up to. Knocking the beehive over but not once getting stung; slipping her tether and wandering into the zoo until being led back by a very bemused zoo director; chasing the chickens around the field, just for a bit of fun. Another time, slipping from her tether and finding her way into the kitchen to help herself to a loaf of bread fresh out of the oven.

Sadly, with working commitments and the children getting older, we could not commit to the high standard of care needed for all the animals we had, and slowly it was phased out. But, what a '*good life*' we had.

Births, Deaths and Marriages

W HAT DID OUR WORK ENTAIL ON A DAILY BASIS?
Cleaning, feeding, checking the health and wellbeing
of our animals and, of course, ensuring the public get value
for the money spent on their admission fee.

Sounds fairly easy on paper, however, the reality was we
had total responsibility for the health and security of every
animal in our care. One error of judgement could have had
long-lasting consequences.

Whatever the weather, animals need care, so we carried
on with our daily routines.

Working in very cold, wet conditions was particularly
hard. Trying to sweep animal droppings, of which there
were plenty, when they are frozen to the ground; cracking
drinking water frozen solid in the troughs; enticing
animals that refuse to leave their warm sleeping quarters,
making it impossible to carry out the cleaning routine. Try
persuading a two-ton rhino that it's genuinely nice out in
the paddock in minus 5 degrees. Memories of continuously

working in the rain in sodden clothes that never seem to dry.

One rather embarrassing incident comes to mind when, being unable to get the key into a frozen lock, I stupidly blew into the lock thinking warm breath would defrost it. How would I explain being unable to move with my lips frozen onto the lock? I had no choice but to tug really hard leaving a fine layer of skin behind. I cannot describe the pain, but lesson learnt.

There are always highs and lows in any line of work, and I would like to share some of those with you.

Starting with my Rhinos, sorry Marwell's Rhinos, OK then, yes; they were and still are my favourites.

Our group consisted of three animals, two females Sula and Kiri, plus Zimba our male. For years Zimba appeared oblivious to any interest the ladies were showing towards him, so eventually it was decided that as part of the breeding programme he would be moved on to another zoo.

Hannu, a stunning boy, was his replacement and after a while, with cautious introductions to our ladies, interest was shown on both sides.

With Rhinos being in season for approximately twelve hours every forty days we could roughly judge when mating would take place, and on a sunny afternoon with a crowd of spellbound visitors watching their every move, a one-hour long mating occurred.

The gestation period is between fifteen and sixteen months, a long wait for her, and for us. Pregnancy kits for rhinos are not readily available in the local chemist so various methods are adopted within the conservation guidelines.

Blood samples... Not easy, distressing for the animal. Poo analyses, much easier, but has to be collected immediately to avoid cross-contamination. Urine sample, easiest of all options but again had to be collected before hitting the floor. Did I say easy?

Thinking cap on...Plan of action. Cutting a forked stick collected from the bridleway I taped a clean plastic drinking cup to it. Explaining to the catering dept my reason for needing empty clean cups, was met with a shake of the head and pitying looks.

After weeks of close surveillance, I noticed Sula ambling over to the spot where she normally pees. With her tail up there wasn't a moment to lose.

In position, akin to a military operation, I slowly eased the cup towards her rear end where, with such force, my highly sophisticated equipment was blasted from my hands hitting the floor and stopping her in mid flow.

Sadly, a sample was never forthcoming, and we had to rely on our observations and knowledge of our animal. With no further matings observed we were as confident as we could be that she was indeed pregnant. With January 1999 as a possible due date, patience would be our virtue.

As her due date became closer regular strolls to the Rhino house became an evening routine.

'*Where are you going at 7pm on Christmas night, Dad?*'

'Where do you think, son,' was the reply.

A chorus of '*Can we come,*' filled the air.

And so, on a cold Christmas evening, warmly wrapped in hand-knitted hats and scarves, we made our way through the bridleway, tree branches glistening with frost, the sound of our footsteps crunching over the frozen ground. The distant calling of Owls in the quiet of the night. Along the South Road we marched, as if on an Arctic adventure, all around us the sounds of nocturnal animal calls echoing in the air.

At last, the Rhino house came into view, and with one last warning to the children not to make a sound, we crept in, holding our breath in nervous anticipation of what we might find... three sleeping Rhinos was the sight that greeted us, that, and the sound of snoring... maybe tomorrow...

Christmas came and went, still no news, maybe tomorrow... New Year's Eve, still no news, maybe tomorrow... End of January, still no news, maybe tomorrow...

Lots of *'maybe tomorrows,'* were thought and said, plus nightly trips to the Rhino House, until... the morning of 8th February, which was, ironically, my day off.

A telephone call from one of my keepers saw me breaking the four-minute mile to get to the Rhino House.

There, settled on a straw bed was the new arrival, alongside a very tired but stroppy mum. I stood in awe, as proud as when my own children were born, before leaving them to bond peacefully. What a special moment and such a privilege.

Later with the sex determined as a male, a name had to be decided on and, as with most births, it was left to the section keepers to make the decision.

We wanted a traditional African name, which was proving rather difficult until we approached the zoo's general manager, Alan, whose son was head of a lifeboat team in South Africa. With his help and that of his crew members, all with different tribal backgrounds, the name *Bhasela* shone through. It meant 'Gift' in the Xhosa language and what a gift he was.

Eventually, the sight of a family group of Rhinos including, by this time a rather large very boisterous baby, charging around the paddock before settling down at mum's side, became a real crowd-pleaser with the public enjoying the spectacle as much as the keepers.

Zoos play an important role in the population management of White Rhinos, both in captivity and in the wild, where they are classed as near threatened. This is mainly due to the threat of poaching for the illegal trade in their horn.

To ensure the absolute best in captive breeding, a dedicated regional stud bookkeeper is appointed by the Association of Zoos and Aquariums. It is their role to register captive animals and to make recommendations for the pairing of animals for breeding. It was time for the decision to be made as to where Bhasela would be most suited as a breeding male.

Flamingo Land Resort, an award-winning zoo in North Yorkshire, was identified as the most suitable. Plans were soon underway to transfer our not so baby Rhino, to pastures new.

Despite their size Rhinos are sensitive animals, particularly to change of routine. With the main objective being to ensure a smooth transition for Bhasela two keepers from Flamingo Land arrived to work with him for a week, to learn his routine and more importantly, for him to get used to them.

Moving day was finally upon us. With a low loader lorry and a high-level crane, with lots of calling and gentle persuasion Bhasela walked calmly into the crate and with a swift but controlled action the door was closed.

Once hoisted onto the low loader, mission accomplished we were good to go.

With Bhasela safely encased onto the back of the lorry, me and our curator, Peter, travelling behind in the Land Rover, we began the two-hundred-mile journey by motorway to North Yorkshire.

Driving at slow speed, cars and lorries flashing by us, I had time to reflect on how I would feel once Bhasela was no longer in my care. Would he miss the sound of my voice? How long before he would be settled with his new keepers? What did the future hold for him?

Finally, we arrived at our destination, tired and hungry but knowing that first and foremost Bhasela had to be settled into his new home.

Again, with a lot of encouragement he carefully inspected his new surroundings, taking in unfamiliar sounds and smells. To give him a sense of reassurance, and if I'm honest myself as well, I stayed with him for some time quietly reassuring him before leaving him to settle.

Saying goodbye to Bhasela was like leaving my children at the school gates on their first day at big school. Unsure what the future would hold for him but happy in the knowledge he would be well looked after.

Another important birth was our Pygmy Hippos, solitary animals, who only tolerate each other for breeding purposes. Their large canine teeth elongate into tusks and are used for defence, making them capable of inflicting deep wounds. Therefore, it is paramount to ensure the female is in season before introducing her to the male.

Holly, the wellington boot assassin, and a young male

named Timbo were together for several years but, sadly, never bred and eventually moved to Krakow Zoo in Poland.

With recommendations from the international stud bookkeeper another pair were identified as being a suitable match for breeding.

Amid great excitement that we may, at last, have a breeding pair of Pygmy Hippos arrangements were soon in place to transfer them from their current home at Whipsnade Zoo in Bedfordshire to us.

The female, Chubbles, was first to arrive, closely followed by the male, Roger.

Both animals settled in well and after a few weeks of careful observations it was noted that Chubbles was becoming very restless and vocal, a sure sign she was in season.

With little known about the breeding behaviour of Pygmy Hippos in the wild, it was decided to let nature take its course and let Chubbles and Roger out together in the paddock. Several matings were observed but with her inflicting a few deep wounds on Roger's side we decided to quickly separate them into their own quarters.

Hippos have smooth, thin skin, to help them stay cool in the humid rainforest. To prevent it drying out in the hot sun it oozes a fluid resembling beads of sweat, it's nature's own sunscreen. With this and a long soak in the pool his wounds quickly healed with no ill effects.

Pygmy Hippos have a gestation period of six months, and with the time drawing ever closer and with Chubbles looking slightly more rounded than usual the holding area was prepared with extra straw to make a soft bed.

As always, our animals kept us on tenterhooks. A careful check first thing every morning was the order of the day.

On one such morning I noticed straw strewn along the inside passage of the house. Quickly, but carefully, closing the sliding door I peeked in to see mum with a black bundle lying closely next to her. My feeling of utter joy suddenly turned to a feeling of sadness as it became obvious the calf was dead.

Regardless of how many times an animal death occurs, apart from a feeling of immense sadness, you always question if anything could have been done to prevent it or was nature taking its course.

Before long Chubbles was pregnant again and with the same preparations in place a healthy calf was born. Named Kenema he grew as strong and boisterous as his mum.

Snow Leopards

WHEN I SHOOK THE HAND OF MR KNOWLES ON THE steps of the Snow Leopard house and accepted his offer of a job I had no idea I would develop such a close bond with these graceful, if solitary, animals.

My first Snow Leopard encounter was with Vilkku, a stunning female. As with any cat, from the smallest domestic to the biggest of the big cats, a soft purr, and in the case of Vilkku, cheek rubbing on the wire fence is a sign of a greeting.

During this time, the daughter of the Finnish studbook keeper was staying with Mr and Mrs Knowles. On visiting the Snow Leopards, she began speaking to Vilkku in her native language, the response was immediate, lots of cheek rubbing along with excited purring. Another new language to master. Along with Japanese I was fast becoming multilingual.

With Snow Leopards being an endangered species in the wild, a conservation captive breeding programme is essential to ensure the future of these magnificent cats. With this in mind, and on recommendations from the stud bookkeeper, a second pair of Snow Leopards currently at another Zoo was identified as being compatible as a breeding pair.

Plans were soon put in place and very soon Vanda, a young female, and Pavel, a handsome looking male, took up residence at Marwell.

With Vanda coming into season soon after their arrival and with mating being observed several times a day, we were hopeful of a successful breeding.

Gestation period for a Snow Leopard is approximately one hundred days and with Vanda's due date becoming ever closer preparations were put in place.

With the cubbing den being cleaned in anticipation and the male separated into a different part of the enclosure from the female, it was now a waiting game.

On one particular morning I crept quietly into the house, closing the door behind me, scared that even a breath of air would disturb the calm. With every nerve in my body on high alert I made my way along the passage to the cubbing den wondering what might lie ahead.

On hearing the sound of squeaking coming from inside the den, with so many different emotions rushing through my mind, I quickly retreated so as not to disturb either mum or babe.

With Mr Knowles waiting patiently outside for news, the huge grin on my face, plus, I admit, rather watery eyes, told him what he wanted to hear, no words were needed.

The sight of my boss and me having a man hug on the steps where I was originally given the job will always stay with me. Hoping we hadn't been seen and with dignity restored we went our separate ways.

Back home that evening, relaxing in front of the fire with a glass of homemade wine, I relayed the day's events to Sandra and the children. The joy of hearing that first squeak from the cubbing den. The man hug with Mr Knowles, which was met with much amusement from the family.

With the night drawing to a close my thoughts were, *I wonder what will tomorrow bring?*

After ten days it was important to ensure all was well with our new arrival, and with Vanda leaving her cub safely within, she ventured to the outside enclosure. With a keeper talking calmly to her, we were able to slide the partition down while I checked on the cub.

Slowly entering the den, wiping my hands in Vanda's urine to pick up mum's scent, I was able to gently pick up the cub and establish it was a healthy boy.

Unexpectedly, a steamroller of emotions hit me; here I was, calmly, holding a ten-day old Snow Leopard cub. What a privilege to be part of a successful breeding programme for these beautiful animals.

Next day it was time to choose a name. As always it was left to the keepers and after much discussion Pavan was the final decision, being a mix of Pavel and Vanda.

With the zoo progressing and a separate Cat section formed, the Snow Leopards were no longer under my care. With a purpose-built enclosure Vanda and Pavel bred once more with Vanda giving birth to two cubs

Although I miss the contact with these magnificent cats, my involvement in the first ever Snow Leopard birth at Marwell fills me with immense pride.

Our Wonderful Public

IT GOES WITHOUT SAYING THAT THE PUBLIC ARE THE life blood of any attraction, with zoos being no exception. Without them zoos could not exist, and valuable conservation work could not continue.

Part of a keeper's role was, and still is, to ensure the public feel they have value for their admission fee, while at the same time promoting the conservation work taking place behind the scenes.

Over the years attitudes towards zoos have changed, with the public being more aware and demanding the very best in animal welfare. Good enclosures must be provided allowing enough space for the animals to roam, mimicking their natural environment as much as possible.

What hasn't changed are the questions and comments we, as keepers, hear day in day out. We are the hands-on animal people who the public rely on to answer their questions... Sometimes about the animals, and sometimes not...

'Where are the toilets?'

'*What time do you close?*'

'*Can we smoke in the zoo?*'

'*How do we get out?*'

Simple questions, easily answered, public happily on their way.

But I have to say there were times when some of the questions warranted a humorous answer.

'*Do you have exit signs?*' I was asked.

'Not very many, like some of our rare animals, they are on the way out.' I replied. With a bemused look and a shake of the head, the member of public walked swiftly away.

'*Excuse me, do you work here?*' Was a question frequently asked while in full uniform and carry two buckets of animal feed. Or... '*Excuse me I'm looking for a keeper, can you help?*'

'*I can't find the elephants, where are they?*' I was abruptly asked by an extremely irate lady.

'Sorry, madam, we don't have elephants.' Was my reply.

An even more abrupt '*Yes, you do!*'

Shoving a road map in my face and pointing to the elephant symbol, I tried to explain it is the commonly used road sign for all zoos and wildlife parks.

'*Well, that's very misleading, I will write a letter of complaint as I came specially to see them.*'

I had a wry smile on my face as I watched her march up to the office to find... *someone in authority!*

'*Excuse me which is the quickest way to get out?*'

I replied, 'Running is the best bet, my friend.' He did smile.

There are of course some that justify belief and you just can't answer.

'*It's rained all day. Where do I go to get my money back?*'

'*It's too hot, where can I get my money back?*'

'*My daughters been stung by a wasp; who can I complain to?*'

'*Why are there no animals here?*'

'*I arrived Christmas Day and you were closed.*'

'*Can I get a lift to the cafeteria my feet are aching?*'

'*It's too crowded why have you let so many people in?*'

'*I hate zoos!*' (My personal favourite)

One day I stopped to watch our new-born Tiger cubs running around the enclosure. Full of fun and mischief, jumping on mum's back until with one sweep of her massive paw they fell to the ground, before getting up and starting again. Amid a lot of Ahhs and Oohs from the public I was pleased to hear a voice behind me saying:

'*Oh my god that's beautiful take a video quick!*' Turning towards them I watched in amazement to discover they were filming a grey squirrel perched on a litter bin.

With a crowd of visitors watching our Rhinos during a one-hour mating several comments were heard.

'*Can I have what you feed them for my husband, please?*'

'*Surely you can stop them; it's not good for my children to see?*'

'*Kids, can you please drag your mother away.*'

'*Kids, can you please drag your father away.*'

Honestly, you couldn't write this stuff... Oh hang, that's exactly what I'm doing right now!

Part of my role was to identify insects and reptiles brought to the zoo by the public. One particular year, there was an influx of false black widow spiders. With the public understandably concerned and with identification difficult over the phone it was my role to reassure them the best I could. The advice they really didn't want to hear was to gently coax it onto a piece of paper and release it as far away from the house as possible. The common reaction being '*I can't I've trod on the bloody thing!*'

One of the most memorable of queries was from the local army depot. While servicing a fleet of vehicles, following a tour of duty to the United States, a number of small black spiders were found. Aware they could be poisonous I thought it best they brought them to the zoo for identification. A little later two military officers arrived tentatively carrying a plastic box. Carefully removing the lid, I looked inside to discover tiny black spiders with the distinctive red hourglass shape mark on their abdomen. Before I could say, 'Yes, definitely Black Widows,' both soldiers had escaped out of the door, last seen running back to the safety of their vehicle.

A common query was one from the local airport. Often came a request for someone to come along to identify a spider found in a consignment of bananas. On one such occasion I arrived at the airport expecting to find the usual stowaway, quiet, harmless, nestled deep within the bunch of under ripe bananas. What I did find, however, was a *Huntsman Spider*, a venomous creature who, when cornered, will defend themselves by rearing up their front legs and showing their fangs. After safely containing the spider and instructing that the consignment should be fumigated in case there were anymore, lurking within, I was on my way. All in a day's work.

Very often I would get calls relating to our own native wildlife. Mainly about creatures found in the house or garden.

'There's a menacing-looking snake with four eyes and a sting on its tail, what is it?' was a common question at the start of spring. Without exception it turned out to be the stunning caterpillar of the Elephant Hawk Moth with its incredible markings.

'I've found what I think is a deadly yellow and black tropical spider in my garden. Is it OK to kill it?'

'NO!' was my rather indignant reply. 'It's a Wasp Spider, fairly common in the South of England. It's totally harmless, enjoy its beauty, please.'

Not everything was confined to invertebrates. Living on site I was on duty for any out-of-hours queries.

On one occasion, after the children had settled for the night, Sandra and I were enjoying the evening's peace when suddenly there was a loud knock on the door.

Not expecting any visitors, I was surprised to find two uniformed police officers on the path.

'Could you come with us, sir,' the larger of the two asked.

I racked my brain to think if I had done anything wrong that could warrant a trip to the police station. I was extremely relieved to be asked to accompany them to the zoo. The police had received several reports from the public that evening that a large black cat, not dissimilar to a Panther, had been sighted running along the road towards Winchester. I was asked to check all the animal enclosures to ensure there were no escapees. Sitting in the back of a police car at midnight with only the headlights to guide us we quietly made our way around the zoo. It was my job to check the locks on every animal enclosure. In and out of the car with only a torch to light the way, while the two policemen remained inside the safety of the car, with the engine running. '*Just in case*,' they said.

With all the animals in their rightful place, no escapes to be reported, I was allowed to return home to the warmth and safety of my bed. As I said, all in a day's (or evening's) work.

Winter Wonderland

WITH TEMPERATURES DROPPING, THE WINTER months have always been the hardest part of the year for any outdoor attractions, zoos being no exception. With visitor numbers dipping, the incentive was to come up with alternative ways to attract people and recoup much-needed income.

So, an idea was formed, with some reservations from the side of the animal keeping staff, to build a Winter Wonderland. Complete with Santa's grotto, it was to be housed on the ground floor of Marwell Hall.

Plans were quickly drawn up. Firstly, a walkway with twinkling fairy lights and fake snow all around. Corridors would be transformed into magical displays of model Arctic animals, penguins skiing down cotton wool mountains, polar bears, with their heads bobbing in tune to music. Santa's little elves would be busy in their workshop, making the many presents ready for Santa to deliver on Christmas Eve.

All this would lead to the long-awaited sight of Santa in his grotto, where each child would be given a gift.

It all sounded good so far. Lights, noise, and excited children encased within the thick stone walls of the Hall, never to be heard. Until…the idea that the miniature train, used to transport visitors around the zoo, was to be turned into a Santa Special, complete with flashing lights, loud music, and noisy, excited children. What started as a good idea was, to me, fast becoming a bit of a nightmare.

With plans afoot for the zoo to stay open until 9pm for twilight visits to the Winter Wonderland, my thoughts turned to the effect this would have on the animals.

How would my Rhinos react to the flashing lights, continuous renditions of Rudolf the Red-Nosed *bloody* Reindeer, booming out from loudspeakers? What would their reaction be to the commotion of screeching, over-excited children as the Santa Special trundled up and down the track, a stone's throw from their sleeping quarters?

With all the keepers being on an evening duty rota during this the festive period, it was going to be easy for me to observe the animals' reactions to such a change in their normal routine.

And so, it began…

After a few skittish moments, the animals appeared eventually to settle well. I was surprised how quickly they adapted to such a change going on around them. In no time at all they ignored the bright-coloured, noisy monster as it made its way back and forth along the track.

No Christmas would be complete without the addition of reindeer… So, I was told!

'*Geoff, we are borrowing two adult reindeer for the children to visit before entering the grotto,*' said Peter the curator. '*We would like your section to look after them.*'

With a tongue-in-cheek thank you, my thoughts turned to even more frozen poo to pick up. So, I wandered away to break the good news to my keepers.

The very next day two fully grown reindeer arrived in all their splendour.

Majestic animals, with an impressive full set of antlers. The bony structures grew from the frontal lobe of the skull like tree trunks with branches fanning out in all directions.

An area was fenced off in front of Marwell Hall to house our two Rudolphs for when they were on Santa duty. Night-time hours were spent in a stable, where they rested on a bed of straw.

Reindeer, though portrayed as gentle animals, soaring through the sky, pulling Santa's sleigh, delivering gifts to well behaved children, in reality are extremely temperamental animals. With their large heavy antlers, used as weapons to defend their territory or harem of females, they warrant some careful handling. As I discovered much to my dismay...

On entering the stable early one morning to rouse the reindeer from their slumber, ready for the day ahead, I was ill prepared for what happened.

With his head down, a guttural roar coming from deep within his throat, the largest male of the two charged towards me. Grabbing his antlers to ward him off proved extremely difficult due to the branch-like structure. I found myself being pinned against the wall, heart thundering, unable to move and with an animal weighing over a hundred kilos pressing me into oblivion. Struggling to breathe and with increasing panic, I was extremely relieved when another keeper who was alerted by the noises coming from the stable, arrived to rescue me.

With the offer of food, Rudolph's attention was distracted from his efforts to kill me. Tentatively, pulling myself to safety, wondering how many of my ribs had been broken, I staggered outside, the fresh air a welcome relief. Looking back into the stable I could see Rudolph contently munching on his food, once again portraying the image of a gentle reindeer leading Santa's sleigh.

With visitor numbers swelling and bookings almost too full to capacity, the atmosphere around the zoo was one of pre-Christmas excitement. Children clutched their wrapped gifts from Santa, in anticipation of what they would find inside.

The Santa Special train adorned in sparkling Christmas decorations was packed full. The sound of laughter rang out all around. Winter Wonderland was a true success for all.

All too soon Christmas Eve arrived and with it the last day of Winter Wonderland – and the busiest! Early in the morning I made my usual journey to the stable, thinking that this was the last time I would have to lead the reindeer down the hill to the hall, their hooves clip-clopping on the frozen ground. They had become a huge attraction to the families waiting their turn to enter the grotto. With the winter sun making its appearance amid the grey clouds, it was with a quiet confidence that I entered the stable. It was the last day, what could possibly go wrong? I said to myself.

But disaster had struck!

At some time during the night the largest of the reindeer had shed one of its most impressive antlers. I could not believe what I was seeing: the bony branches lying on the straw bed. Was this really happening?

Time for an emergency meeting.

With everyone involved in the smooth running of Winter Wonderland being summoned to the Hall, the meeting commenced.

Like an emergency committee formed in time of war, the debate began on how we were going to disguise the fact Rudolph only had one antler. Amid cries of, *'It's our last day and we are fully booked'*. Some rather interesting suggestions were put forward:

'Why don't we put a false red nose on him to distract people from noticing his missing antler?' said a member of the office staff (who will remain nameless!).

'Can he stand behind the other reindeer, so it doesn't show?'

With all further suggestions discounted, the only option was to continue his duties as normal and act as if nothing had happened.

For the rest of the day, with Rudolph looking not quite so majestic and slightly lopsided, the show went on.

Later that evening, with Winter Wonderland at a close and the animals settled for the night, it was time to reflect. Walking back home, almost in a trance, my mind trying to take in what was so different, I realised it was the silence. No music. No noisy, excited children. No sound of the train clattering along the track.

Just peace...an almost eerie silence.

Due to the popularity of that very first Winter

Wonderland, it was to become an annual event. As each year passed it grew bigger and better: an army of volunteers, resplendent in their roles as Christmas characters; Mother Christmas gave out sweets to the children and tried to keep the naughty elves in order; adults were willingly plied with mince pies and mulled wine. We had to place two Santas, in separate grottos, to cope with the ever-increasing flow of children eagerly awaiting their gifts. A tractor disguised as a road train, more flashing lights, and ever-increasing, noisy children and, of course, the continuous rendering of Christmas music.

Reindeer – this time with antlers intact. Craft stalls selling hand-made wares, food stalls, sending an aroma of hot dogs and burnt onions wafting through the air.

My favourite of all the stalls was the one selling Dunkin' Donuts. How could I resist the sweet, sugary smell as they hit the hot oil? Covered in sugar they became a teatime treat for the keepers on section.

As with all good things, Winter Wonderland came to an end. The amount of time and manpower it was taking each year was no longer sustainable. A much smaller, but just as good, Christmas event replaced it. Complete with road train and reindeer. Did I miss the annual journey into a magical kingdom of make-believe? The honest answer is – no. Too much upheaval for both the keeping staff and, more importantly, the animals. But I did miss the Dunkin' Donuts.

Ghostly Goings-On

SITUATED IN A CENTRAL POSITION OVERLOOKING THE zoo stands the magnificent, Grade 2 listed, medieval Marwell Hall. It was built around 1320 by Walter Woodlock, a relative of the Bishop of Winchester. From the sixteenth century the Hall was owned by the Seymour family and it is reputed that King Henry VIII married Jane Seymour in the great hall at precisely the time Anne Boleyn, his second wife, was being beheaded at the Tower of London. In 1638 the Hall was bought from the Seymour family by Sir Henry Mildmay, an associate of King Charles I.

Over the years Marwell Hall and the surrounding land changed hands on many occasions, until in 1969 when it was purchased by Mr John Knowles and consequently became Marwell Zoo, as it is known to this day.

With so much history dating back to the fourteenth century and beyond, it is little wonder reports of ghostly happenings have been plentiful. It is reputed that the most famous, the ghost of Anne Boleyn, stalks the corridors of Marwell Hall plotting revenge on Jane Seymour.

The most well-travelled of ghost stories is one of the mistletoe brides. While playing a game of hide-n-seek on her wedding day the bride hid in a chest which locked from the outside. Despite the groom and guests searching every room in the Hall her cries went unheard leaving her imprisoned until her remains were discovered many years later. Was Marwell Hall the setting for such a tragic tale? Does the young bride haunt the corridors? We will never know.

What we do know is that within the shadows of its long winding corridors and empty rooms with their creaking floorboards and hidden corners the daily running of the zoo took place, telephones ringing, and office staff hard at work, all around them distant whispers of times gone by. The great hall dominates the lower floor, with its wood panelling and large stone fireplace lending itself to remind us of times past, when both gentry and royalty resided. Shadows seen of ladies in all their grandeur and gentlemen with their breeches and long coats, entertaining their guests with vast banquets long into the night.

During the early days of the zoo, 'The Hall' as it was commonly known was home to Mr and Mrs Knowles, the zoo director and his wife. They occupied four rooms on the middle floor, accessed by a sweeping staircase which itself has been the centre of many unexplained happenings.

The sudden icy chill on a warm summer day, footsteps heard when no one else was around, a feeling that you are not alone. All these things were and probably still are, experienced by a number of individuals. At one point Mr Knowles, acutely aware of the rumours and himself experiencing a feeling of unease in the vicinity of the staircase, advised his cleaner to use the other staircase at the front of the house.

The top floor of the Hall was used for storage and was accessed by a dark, steep, stone stairway, leading to a variety of small attic rooms. It is rumoured these rooms were once used by smugglers to hide their contraband. There have been reports of the sound of barrels being rolled across the floor and voices being heard in the quiet of the night. Compared to the grandeur of the rest of the house those rooms had the feeling of neglect, dimly lit with a damp musty odour, rendering them abandoned and lifeless. But still with the aura of history and a little imagination, the past could come rushing back.

Among the many items stored within the rooms were props from the zoos annual Christmas event, Winter Wonderland. Life-size figures of snowmen, penguins skating on ice, Santa's little elf helpers, all covered in dust sheets giving the appearance of ghostly silhouettes. One of the rooms was used by the education department to breed mice. At weekends it fell to my section to check and feed them. Not one to succumb to ghostly tales of things that go bump in the night I will admit to feeling a little uneasy when climbing the stairs, wondering what lay beyond. Of course, I could have delegated, but always being one to lead by example I felt it was my duty to carry out this task. However, I was always alert to the fact that one of my team would find it amusing to creep up behind me. I am pleased to say this didn't happen. The sight of their quivering head keeper wouldn't have been very dignified.

Many ghostly happenings had been reported both in and outside the hall. On two occasions the doors had locked trapping staff members inside the rooms when it was proven no one had been in the vicinity. Apparitions of a shimmering figure in a Puritan robe, at first just a hint of mist, walking amongst the shadows in the corridor, before disappearing through a wall. Items in a locked room, with only one person having a key, have been reported to have moved some distance from where left.

People reported the feeling of something or someone watching from the shadows.

The grounds surrounding the Hall had not escaped reports of ghostly goings-on. The back lawn in particular has been the focus of many reported sightings as have the row of trees just beyond known as Yew Tree Walk.

During the English Civil War (1642–1651) Marwell Hall was the site of a skirmish between the Roundheads, who at the time were staying at the Hall, and a group of Royalists who were staying close by in Winchester. Despite being outnumbered, the Roundheads were defeated, resulting in many casualties. It has been reported that a headless Cavalier astride a white horse has been seen galloping across the back lawn. The sound of horse's hooves travelling far into the distance. A lady in Tudor attire had also been seen walking across the back lawn. Could it be Jane Seymour or Ann Boleyn? No one will ever know.

Considering myself to be a level-headed person, I have on several occasions had reason to question my reluctance to believe in the paranormal. Over time I have personally encountered several unexplained experiences that will always stay in the back of my mind.

The South Road housed two beautiful European lynx, stunning, medium-sized cats both with attitude. Their enclosure backed onto dense woodland with its gnarled old trees and the cloying aroma of decomposing leaves which even in daylight gave off a sense of isolation.

Normal daily routine was to shut both cats in their inside den while cleaning the outside area. On more than one occasion while carrying out the routine a sixth sense of being watched would come over me, the urge to look behind was overwhelming. On the occasions I did, I would feel or catch a glimpse of something, or someone vanish from my line of vision.

My first thought was that someone was hiding, playing games on me, but even when I shouted out, akin to playing a game of hide-n-seek, I just knew there was no one there.

Speaking with one of my keepers, Simon, a very down to earth, practical person, he admitted he had experienced the same sensation on more than one occasion.

Despite my previous experiences I was determined to keep an open mind, however any misgivings I had totally disappeared following my next encounter.

South Road housed a small group of African Kudu, one, a stunning male named Duke kept his girls, and sometimes us in order. With an impressive three twists in his large horns, you didn't argue. We both knew who was boss in his domain.

One morning around eight thirty I began the daily routine of cleaning their indoor quarters. While putting down fresh bedding I heard children's voices coming from outside. My first thought was that I was running very late or that a school group had come in very early. Fearing the latter, I headed outside to ensure the public barrier was in place. Once outside the voices suddenly stopped. Thinking the wind had carried the sound from the village school and with a shrug of the shoulders I carried on with my work. A few minutes later the same voices again with no sign of children.

By the third time of this happening, I was beginning to be a little perplexed and on remembering it was Sunday and not a school day, I must admit to feeling spooked.

Later that morning I related my experience to Simon who gave a wry smile and nodded; enough said. This incident became quite a regular occurrence eventually becoming an acceptable if not strange part of the morning routine.

The only explanation to my next encounter was that I, without doubt, had seen a ghost.

We had, at the time, two beautiful young Black Rhinos housed in a purpose-built building with two separate indoor areas. After letting our male, Kes, outside and with the female, Katie, remaining inside I began the morning cleaning routine. Within seconds an icy chill had seeped through the house. Staring into the distance Katie suddenly began turning in circles, snorting, mouth open as if overwhelmed by terror. As I turned it felt as if all the air had been sucked out of the building and coming towards me as if in mid-air was what I can only describe as a shimmering grey cigar shape about four foot in height. Time stood still as it hovered over me before slowly moving away and disappearing through the wall. Now, I'm not really one to imagine these things, but the fact that the rhino sensed it first made me really believe something unexplainable had happened in that moment. Eventually a feeling of calm came over the house but with a heightened sense of awareness it took some time for both of us to settle. I checked every possible scenario that came into my confused mind, but nothing really convinced me that this was my imagination playing tricks. It never happened again but to this day I know what I saw.

And then of course, there was the old cottage, our home.

Being in the grounds of the Marwell Hall estate and with evidence of the surrounding land dating back to the Roman times, our cottage was also rumoured to be haunted however, we did not experience anything untoward until work started on the foundations for a ground floor extension.

From that day strange things occurred, lights turning on and off, the sound of footsteps, rooms suddenly becoming icy cold sending shivers up and down your spine. The sound of something or someone being dragged across the floor upstairs when everyone was downstairs.

Trying to make light of it so as not to scare the children I thought I had succeeded until one day Angela who was then four years old, refused to go into the newly built dining room.

'The old lady keeps telling me to be quiet and go to bed,' she said, describing a white-haired lady in a long black frock sitting in the corner of the room.

Believing she had heard our muted conversations about ghosts we thought she would have forgotten about it the next day… how wrong we were.

Not long after, Angela was alone in the dining room when I overheard her saying 'I don't want to go to bed.' Asking her who she was talking to she said, 'The old lady.'

As time went on the conversations between Angela and the *old lady* became less frequent until, one day, stopping altogether. Many years later our granddaughter Leah, Angela's daughter, then aged four, refused to go into the dining room as there was an old lady telling her to '*be quiet and go to bed*'.

Strange happenings were not confined to the inside of the cottage. The land surrounding the cottage dates back to the ancient Saxon times. There is evidence of an Iron Age settlement dating back to the Romans in the nearby village of Owslebury.

Local legend has it that a medieval monastery was situated close to the grounds of the Marwell Estate. There were many reports of ghostly figures being seen in the vicinity.

Both our sons, Aron and Vincent, described seeing figures dressed in monks' habits, shimmering, slightly out of focus, standing at the bottom of the field then disappearing as if they were never there.

While walking along the lane close to the cottage after visiting a friend in the village Aron reported seeing a man walking slowly towards him.

Thinking it might be a visitor from the zoo Aron carried on walking. As the man got closer Aron said his shape appeared to change, going slowly out of focus before disappearing altogether. Aron, although not being one to be easily frightened, ran the reminder of the way home.

Despite all this we never felt threatened or uneasy. Our home was our sanctuary, and in time we came to accept that maybe we were sharing it with the spirit world, and that was fine.

Do I believe in ghosts? I like to think there is a logical explanation for all the things I have seen and heard but, quite honestly, I can think of nothing logical to explain my own experiences and that of my family whilst living at Marwell.

Close to Extinction

THE OUTBREAK OF FOOT AND MOUTH DISEASE IN THE South of England in 2001 was a major disaster for all animal-based establishments. Marwell Zoo was no exception. Nearby farms were forced to put up exclusion zones and as the ban on any animal movement within the UK took hold, stringent safeguarding plans were put in place throughout the zoo.

Disinfectant foot baths at all animal house entrances and more importantly at the zoo entrance where every vehicle entering also had their tyres sprayed.

As an extra precaution all keeping staff were issued with very fetching blue one-piece suits to cover their normal work uniform.

As cases increased in the local area the first mass cull of farm animals took place. Lorry loads of sheep and cattle were slaughtered. I couldn't begin to imagine the devastation this would have on the farming community.

Following government guidelines and advice from the vet the difficult decision was made to close the zoo to the general public.

Just because the zoo was closed to the public our daily routine of feeding, cleaning and general husbandry couldn't stop. Our regime carried on as normal, with very little impact apart from the eerie silence.

No screaming children, the road and rail train silenced, no public milling around. Almost like a ghost town, the silence was deafening.

The animals appeared unsettled, particularly the Rhinos, picking up on the atmosphere, the silence, the figures in blue coming in to clean them out, their feet sloshing about in troughs of strange smelling liquid. I tried my best to reassure them, calmly talking to them as I made my way in and out of the houses, but I could tell they were as confused and unsettled as I was.

The future of the zoo was in doubt; back then the cost of running the zoo amounted to £7500 a day. With no money coming in from public admissions the situation was close to reaching crisis point.

All staff took a wage cut and the director waived his salary. This made little difference. As time went on and with little or no sight in end to the epidemic, it became clear Marwell itself was on the brink of extinction, just like many of the animals in its care.

The feeling of impending gloom reverberated around the whole of the zoo, from keepers to office staff to management everyone was dreading the day the zoo would close its gates for the last time.

What would happen to all the animals, where would they go?

Thinking practically, without my job, how would I look after my family, what would become of us? We would have to leave the cottage, our home we had all grown to love. So many unanswered questions, we just didn't know.

Despite the constant worry, the animal care and welfare came first. Their routine had to continue, and it was my job as head keeper to try to keep up the morale of my staff. Not an easy task when I was struggling with my own.

With no food outlets open within the zoo, once a week I would order takeaway pizza to be delivered at lunch time for the section. A small gesture but it made a welcome change from sandwiches and crisps.

As the epidemic reached over a thousand cases and still with no end in sight, contingency plans were being made for the impending possibility of re-homing as many animals as we could. Given the climate at the time, other zoos were feeling the strain as much as we were. It was just a matter of weeks until that dreaded day would be upon us until…

Up stepped an army of volunteers determined to keep the zoo open and the animals safe at all costs. Like an army of wartime volunteers with their brightly coloured buckets they descended on every major outlet within miles. Standing outside supermarkets in all weathers, waving the buckets under the noses of disconcerting shoppers, begging them to contribute to keep Marwell open. Besieging local radio and television stations who welcomed them with open arms ready and willing to take up the cause, they showed images of as many cute and cuddly animals as they could to tug on the heart and purse strings of their listeners.

Out of the impending gloom came a glimmer of hope. Donations started trickling in; each day increasing until extra office staff had to be drafted in to keep up with the daily influx of post.

From elderly people donating some of their pension to school children giving up their pocket money, the support rolled in. As the donations increased so did the publicity. More and more people wanted to join in the fundraising. Cake sales, pub quizzes, the village school and WI came up with inventive ways to raise funds. Everyone joined together to help the cause. And still the army of volunteers stood out in all weathers waving their brightly coloured buckets.

There was a change in the atmosphere around the zoo; everyone was in a more buoyant mood. With smiling faces, a renewed energy gave hope for the future.

Six weeks on and with cases slowly decreasing around the county, the decision was made to re-open the zoo, but still with stringent precautions in place.

Any visitors from highly affected areas would not be allowed in, their postcodes being checked by car parking staff. At the zoo entrance there were foot baths in place for the public to use before they could enter. Soggy shoes were the order of the day, a small price to pay for the safety of the animals. We wondered how that would go down, but the public hopefully would understand and accept this, a small price to pay for the zoo's safety and the pleasure they had visiting.

With the date of the grand re-opening announced on local television and radio we all waited with bated breath to welcome back our visitors. I hoped, as we all did, that people would support us.

Slowly but surely cars started to appear along the lane, making their way to the car park until every space was occupied. A feeling of euphoria replaced the worry and stress of the past few months.

The zoo was once again bursting with excited children. The road and rail trains trundling up and down the track. The joy of being asked, '*Where are the toilets?*' Never again would I find myself losing patience with our wonderful public.

Slowly things started to return to normal, restrictions lifted, no more blue overalls or foot baths.

My family safe and secure once more. As much as I tried to hide the severity of the situation, it did have an impact on Sandra and the children. They were as worried about me as I was about them.

Throughout all this our fantastic army of volunteers rose to the challenge, never faltering in their quest to save our zoo. They will never realise it was not just the animals and the zoo, it was a whole lot more they helped save, and for that I will always be truly thankful.

Tropical House

YOU MAY HAVE GATHERED BY NOW MY PASSION HAS always been for invertebrates, reptiles, and amphibians.

In the early days at Marwell, tortoises and a few snakes in the education centre, mainly used for talks, were the closest I ever got to working with reptiles. I lived in hope that one day a few more species would be added. Imagine my joy when our director and curator uttered the words:

'Do you think we could do with more of these kinds of animals?'

It took less than a millisecond to agree with them, already, mentally, writing a list of must-haves. At last, the opportunity I had been waiting for was about to materialise.

The semi-aquatic house, home to Tapirs and Pygmy Hippos, was the ideal start in providing the right warm, humid conditions necessary for most species of reptile.

With the house already home to some amazing tropical plants the decision was made to turn one end of the public area into an exhibit for a rather beautiful Red-tailed boa constrictor, named Nakira, who was fast growing out of her home in the education centre.

A good-sized area with a sliding patio door was constructed. Inside was a water container large enough for Nakira to cool down in, and branches to climb and rub against when shedding her skin. There was room for her to stretch and move, a good start to what I hoped would become a great reptile section.

With Nakira secured in a container, amid a lot of fond goodbyes from the education staff, we made the short journey to the semi-aquatic house and her new home. She soon settled in, wrapping her long body around the branches before slithering her way through the undergrowth to explore her new surroundings.

As the concerns regarding the loss of vast acres of tropical rainforests increased worldwide, and the fact that other zoos had existing tropical exhibits, Marwell turned its thoughts to a tropical house. The onus being on telling the story of the destruction of the rainforest and the effect it was happening on wildlife in general.

At this time funds were not available for such a huge investment but then, by a massive stroke of luck, a tropical glass house became available at an affordable price from Windsor Safari Park.

The most suitable site for this massive 90ft × 56ft building was in the grounds of the old stable yard, which I'm pleased to say was part of my section.

With a professional company assigned, the huge structure was delivered. It was soon built, along with fitted automatic blinds for shade, a filtered misting system and the all-important twin boiler heating system. The planting of the many tropical plants began. With Sue overseeing the work, the beginnings of a tropical rainforest took shape.

The invertebrate exhibits were left for me to design, glass vivariums in position, furnished with branches, logs, and plants transforming them into mini rainforests. With lighting and heating added by Phil, our in-house electrician, all that was left for me to do was to fill them with some rare and beautiful species.

Like Noah and the Ark, the animals came in two by two, starting with Jungle Scorpions, followed by Madagascan Hissing Cockroaches, Millipedes, Stick Insects, and my own Tarantula, donated to the cause.

Tall exhibits were built to house tree-dwelling species. A stunning Jackson's Chameleon with his three facial horns, quickly followed by Burmese Pythons one of the larger snake species. Things were moving at a nice pace. A large exhibit of Amazon Poison Dart Frogs with a waterfall and pool added movement and colour amongst the green of the foliage. Later a South American species of Butterfly, the Red Postman, so named for its vibrant colour joined the frogs, flitting gracefully among the green of the tropical plants. Another deciding factor to add them was their unique ability to fly backward, unlike most butterflies, therefore they would not be harmed by the glass.

To add to the collection a young West African Dwarf Crocodile, with attitude, duly arrived from Bristol Zoo. This became a firm favourite with staff and visitors alike.

A large tank with a filter system became the home of

the impressive Red-bellied Piranha, always a talking point for outrageous claims, they will strip your hand in seconds if you put it in, being the common one. Transferring them from container to tank should have been simple but in the unlikely event you have to do this, never, ever, use a standard fish hand net as they have a tendency to bite straight through it making them rather awkward to pick up. Fingers intact we completed the task; all that was left to do was change out of very wet clothes and mop the floor.

The central island was home to a pair of Pygmy Marmosets, stunning but shy South American primates. With their purpose-built house and a large fully leaved tree we hoped they would settle and not try to cross the surrounding pool which housed a Pacu. The Pacu is a relative to the Piranha family, but without the aggressive personality, preferring a diet of fruit and veg rather than flesh.

After several days of regular observation, we all agreed the Marmosets had decided to stay exactly where they were. We will never know if that was due to them being settled or the sight of a Pacu waiting below.

With Sue, myself and the team working together, albeit with a lot of banter, mainly plants vs animals, and with an off-show area for breeding and quarantine completed, we were soon open, ready for our visiting public.

A huge favourite of mine has always been leaf cutter ants. After much research we managed to obtain a nucleolus colony from Central South America, known as parasol ants, aptly named due to them carrying cut leaves above their heads ready to take back to their nest where they are turned into pulp and later fungus for food.

First and foremost was the building of a low walled exhibit with a moat to stop the ants from escaping.

Or so we thought... A procession of ants with green umbrellas, making their way back and forth to the nest is a sight to behold until... when night fell and all was quiet and dark, they succeeded in bridging the moat and going for an overnight jolly into the tropical house, munching their way through Sue's beloved plants. An early morning call from Sue meant only one thing... I was in trouble.

'Come and get these bloody ants away from my plants.'

Without further ado, like the cape crusader on a rescue mission, I ran to the tropical house, fear cursing through my veins, dreading what I would find. All those very expensive and important plants with their leaves stripped bare, only the skeletal stems remaining?

The relief I felt when I discovered that only a few leaves had been chewed was immense and with my heart rate returning to normal I managed to round up as many ants as I could and return them to their enclosure where they could deposit their ill-gained spoils. Not an easy task, but easier than pacifying Sue. This happened on many an occasion as the colony grew. After several modifications we decided to rectify the problem with a series of acrylic tubes made for the ants to walk through, which in turn led to a separate feeding tank. Problem solved, everyone happy. This was without a doubt one of the highlights of my career.

Full Circle

LIKE ALL LARGE ORGANISATIONS, CHANGES TO working practices are commonplace, zoos being no exception.

Plans were being made to rearrange the animal sections into more specialist areas, with staff being relocated in line with both their interests and their skill set.

It had been mentioned a few times to me that a section for the specific care of invertebrates, reptiles and amphibians would be beneficial. Following a formal meeting with the curator, I was given the go ahead. This new section would be located in the Tropical House and I would hold the position of head keeper, in charge of... well, just myself.

Despite being excited at the prospect of this new venture I was sorry to be leaving my team and animals, particularly the Rhinos. Thankfully, they were within walking distance of the Tropical House making it easy for me to visit.

Exchanging my bass yard broom for a much smaller dustpan and brush I entered my domain, a lush green tropical jungle, the air laden with moisture, the gentle sound of water cascading down rocks before landing in the pool below.

Standing quietly, listening to the sounds of the rainforest, a sense of belonging came over me and at that moment I knew this was exactly where I wanted to be. My boyhood dream had come true.

Later in the day I was joined by Sue, now head of plants, she was just as equally excited about our new venture. Having a sound working relationship as well as a firm friendship the banter soon began.

'You're not going to touch my plants, are you?'

'No, only the important inhabitants of the house, all the green stuff is yours,' was my reply.

With my working routine taking shape, it was time to concentrate on how I could improve the section and what new species to add to the collection. *'What conservation breeding programmes could I become involved in?'* I wondered. The opportunities were endless and with that in mind I began approaching other zoos to discuss my plans.

To my delight I was asked to represent Marwell as a member of the Taxon Advisory Group, or TAG for short. TAG is an association of zoos and aquariums, their primary objectives being to manage, and support sustainability and conservation needs for the management of vulnerable species of mammals, birds, amphibians, reptiles, and invertebrates. Oops, almost forgot, plants as well, Sorry, Sue!

Among the various exhibits of reptiles and fish which, although under my care, were allocated in different areas around the zoo, were two extremely aggressive bull snakes, a large aquarium housing Malawi cichlid, and a few tortoises, which required daily checks. With my workload increasing and plans for future expansion it was becoming clear a second staff member was required. Several interviews later Dan, an extremely knowledgeable and enthusiastic young man, was appointed to join the team.

Now there were two of us it gave me the opportunity to attend the next TAG meeting being held at London Zoo. With preparation in hand the day of the TAG meeting duly arrived.

I found myself jostling for space on an early morning crowded commuter train from Winchester to Waterloo. The journey ran on, as the open space and green fields,

I had become accustomed too turning slowly into concrete buildings. The train rattled its way along the track before finally stopping at its destination.

The hustle and bustle of Waterloo station was unfamiliarly overwhelming, with so many people running, oblivious to everything and everyone around them, distorted voices booming out the tannoy, giving instructions nobody understands.

There was standing room only on the bus to Camden Town, everyone moving in sequence, like ants hurrying to reach their destinations.

How I preferred my new shorter commute to work, through green fields, cleaner, fresher air, void of traffic and noise.

Reaching the zoo and with time to spare I was instantly drawn to the site of the old Insect House, where I felt nostalgia for the days gone by and the people I had worked with, not forgetting the opportunity given to me to fulfil my boyhood dream.

The Insect House as I remembered it, was no longer there, taking its place was an amazing new complex, and aptly named B.U.G.S, short for Biodiversity Underpinning Global Survival. An impressive building, tailor-made for the important conservation work carried out. I wonder if they used the same old brown teapot. Somehow, I doubted it.

With the meeting underway first on the agenda was plans for the creation of a breeding programme for the critically endangered Fregate Island beetle, from the Seychelles, fast facing extinction. They were one of the world's most threatened animal species and it was with great honour I was asked to take part in a captive breeding programme. It would give Marwell the recognition it deserved.

All breeding programmes have husbandry guidelines that aim to promote high standards in animal care. A fine line was, and still is, created between providing good environmental conditions to recreate their natural habitat, both for the well-being of the animal and to encourage breeding. The creation of an interesting and educational exhibit for the public, to enable us to get the very important message of conservation across is just as important.

Being part of such an important breeding programme came with great responsibility, something that both Dan and I embraced. We were confident in both our ability and the support of a wider team at London Zoo. The breeding programme went exceptionally well. With improvements to our section and good feedback from the public we were quickly being taken seriously by other zoos. Before long we were promised another breeding programme, this time

Kleinman's or as they are more commonly known, Egyptian tortoises.

These reptiles are originally from Egypt and Libya and with a combination of habitat loss and overcollecting by the illegal pet traders, their numbers were dwindling closer and closer to extinction. With a carefully created breeding programme being their only hope, we were keen to contribute and set to work on creating a small, heated, sandy area within the tropical house, where they subsequently settled well. They were a huge hit with the public providing us the opportunity to explain about the importance of the conservation work being carried out.

As time went on, another section restructure occurred and with it the opportunity to take over the large building that was once part of the old children's zoo. With the extra work of designing and building seven new, larger enclosures, the ongoing success of our breeding programmes and the continuous monitoring and recording of each individual in the stud book, a third member of staff, Rob, was appointed, and now we were three.

With the new building complete we were able to move the Kleinman's tortoises into a new, more spacious home. It was great to see them running around, yes running, they can move fast when they see food.

Following the success of previous breeding programmes, we were asked to be a part of a further two, the Beaded Lizard and the Gila Monster Lizard.

Both are very colourful species that can be found in Mexico, they are also the only lizards to have their own method of delivering venom by chewing their prey and then running the venom along a grove into the wound. Careful handling was a top priority.

One of the most popular exhibits with the public was my nemesis, black widow spiders. With now extremely strict guidelines anti-venom was kept on site, securely locked away. No more need for the awaiting feather quill.

The building was aptly named Cold-blooded Corner, which I'm sure enticed people in, and at times, out very quickly! The brave folks who remained appeared enticed by our selection of animals and good-size enclosures, all beautifully planted out by Sue. As our Cold-blooded Corner became more and more popular with the public, daily keeper talks were introduced with snakes and spiders as the main attraction.

With limited space in the house there was no need for a microphone and with my confidence growing I found that interacting with the public on a subject I was passionate about was a sincerely enjoyable experience. Animal welfare was paramount, with numerous species of snakes and seven Chile rose tarantulas, all females, and all named Rosie, we were able to rotate them on a daily basis.

We really knew that we had been accepted into the conservation breeding and reintroduction programme when, following a telephone call from the B.U.G.S department at London Zoo, we were asked to be a part of the international breeding programme for Partula snail. These are tiny land snails from the Polynesian islands and the objective of the programme was to reintroduce them back into the wild.

Dear reader, before you yawn and skip this episode, please let me explain.

Partula are part of a group of critically endangered snails; out of 77 species, 51 are now extinct in the wild and only 11 of these survive in captivity. Their demise was caused by the introduction of giant land snails to the islands as a food source for the inhabitants, however, they quickly became a crop pest to local farmers. To combat this carnivorous species of snail, the Florida Rosy Wolf snail was introduced with the hope that these would feed on the giant land snails. However little thought had gone into this, as giant land snails reach eight inches in length and the wolf snails only reaching three. Needless to say, the Partula became the unintentional food source of the wolf snail, resulting in disastrous consequences.

With London Zoo being at the forefront of the international breeding programme, we worked with them to set up a room carefully designed and dedicated to these tiny creatures. With strict husbandry guidelines and everything in place, two species arrived – one of which was extinct in the wild. Looking into a tank housing the only snails of this species in existence brought home to me the vital work carried out by organisations around the world to bring wildlife back from the brink.

While on a royal engagement to officially open the zoo's new lemur complex, the Princess Royal, Princess Anne was asked if she would like to visit the Partula snail breeding area. Having met her before at the opening of the Penguin World complex, where she showed a great interest in everything we were doing, I was sure our snails would be as much of a delight to her. After practising my *mam as in jam* speech, she arrived. Following introductions, I set about explaining, with great enthusiasm, our role in this especially important project. I do hope her Royal Highness found our snails as attractive as the lemurs. Sadly, I have my doubts.

With our snails breeding, a slow process (giving birth to one baby every three months), we felt confident our contribution would go some way to securing the future of this tiny animal.

As the years galloped by, what started as the Tropical House and me, had become a major attraction within the zoo. With animal numbers swelling, a fourth member of staff was appointed. With an increase in paperwork, staff rotas, health and safety and the never-ending risk assessments, I found myself tied to the computer rather than doing what I enjoy and do best, hands-on animal husbandry. I did, however, feel a great sense of achievement from my days as a tea boy and sweeper in the Insect House at London Zoo all the way to head keeper at Marwell with my own invertebrate section. A lot had happened in between, but it truly felt as if I had gone full circle.

End of a Dream

AFTER ALMOST FIFTY YEARS WORKING IN MY DREAM job, the time came to hand the reins to someone new. With new ideas and management changes, retirement beckoned.

It was hard to imagine not waking up to the sound of early morning birdsong. No more walking to work along the bridleway, greeting the wildlife that accompanied me on my journey. No more early morning meetings with my team, tea poured from the old brown teapot whilst planning our day ahead.

It was hard to say goodbye to work colleagues who had become friends over the years. We promised to stay in touch but knew that was probably unlikely.

It was even harder to leave the company of the incredible animals I had been so privileged to work with. My whole career had been a privilege and not just a job.

Had my work ethics made a difference to the smooth running of the zoo? Maybe a little, in a modest way. Would

I be remembered in years to come? Probably not. Will I remember some of the amazing people I have worked with? Yes, I think I most definitely will. Was I going to miss the forever increasing meetings, taking over a great chunk of my working day, the endless paperwork that went with them? No. I certainly would not.

Throughout my career I have been hands-on. Preferring a bucket and brush to an office surrounded by reams of paperwork and spreadsheets.

So how did I feel on my last working day? Sadness, of course. Knowing it would be my last working day with my animals.

When I entered the Rhino house, and gave Sula, my favourite, the last of my polo mints which she had become so used to having over the years, I watched her salivate with sheer pleasure. Knowing someone else would be looking after her, would they give her their last polo mint?

Saying goodbye to my team, I hoped some of the things I had taught them would keep them in good stead for years to come.

Clearing my spare uniform from my locker I thought, never again would Sandra have to wash and dry it to rid it of the Guanaco spit.

I then made my way to the office to hand in my keys and radio. That's when the tears formed, as I walked out of the zoo gates, trying hard not to look back.

Realisation setting in that I was, from that moment on, a retired zookeeper.

Would the future be as exciting as the past?

With all the children now adults and with families of their

own it was time for Sandra and me to start a new chapter in our lives. But how could we leave our home, the place our children grew up in? The woods where the children played and had adventures, the camps they built, the sound of laughter as they ran freely amongst the trees and tall grasses. So many adventures, so many memories.

Our first task was to find somewhere to live. With the cottage, being tied accommodation with the job, we were given three months' notice to vacate it.

So began the search for our new home.

Almost to the day of the three-month deadline a bungalow became available in a village, just north of Winchester. After one viewing, we decided it would be the ideal place to make our new home.

Much smaller than the cottage, with just one bedroom, we discovered the true meaning of *down-sizing*. What should we take with us? What could we leave behind?

The old, frayed, doormat, engrained with mud. A testimony of the many boots wiped clean over the years. It had to come with us. The garden pots, lovingly painted, and restored adding a splash of colour on a grey winter day. The six-foot flower pot man, I had made many years ago. Now cracked in places, he still sat, just as majestically as guardian of the garden. He was definitely coming with us.

The last evening in our old home soon arrived. With a roaring fire in the grate, a glass of wine in hand, and packing boxes all around us Sandra and I sat reminiscing about our life in the country.

Amid a lot of laughter and a few tears the memories came flooding back.

There was the first time I attempted to light a fire, almost having to call the fire brigade.

My first and last attempt to sweep the chimney with brushes borrowed from a friend, the first brush getting firmly stuck halfway up. Rushing out to buy a set of new brushes. Trying to dislodge the one firmly stuck. Three attempts, and a further new set of brushes and the chimney was finally swept. We decided that job was best left to the professionals in future.

Then there was the day the goat found her way into the kitchen, helping herself to the loaf of bread, fresh out of the oven. Sandra wasn't amused!

The children coming home from playing in the woods, tired and hungry, covered in mud. This brought back memories of my own childhood when it was safe to play out on the streets of London.

The village life we all embraced. The friends we made. And what fun we had taking part in the village pantomime. Learning our lines, going over and over them in rehearsals, never quite getting them right on the opening night to the delight of the audience. Where would we be without village pantomimes?

Winters where the snow lay thick, making the lanes impassable. Taking the children to and from school on the back of the zoo tractor. Collecting more children from the neighbouring farms along on the way. What an adventure that was.

The next day before quietly closing the door for the very last time I looked around the empty shell of our home. A feeling of sadness swept over me. Where had all the years gone?

Shaking off the feelings of nostalgia, I began the journey to Winchester and our new home. A journey along the same lanes as that day so long ago when I travelled to Marwell for my interview, the branches of the trees still overhung, a little older, a little more gnarled and knotted. Through the village, passing the church, the same pub but with a different name. Sadly, the village shop was no more, replaced by a new house. Time does move on.

Arriving at our new home I found Sandra, who had arrived earlier in the day, sitting amongst a sea of packing boxes. Wondering where on earth she was going to put all the things we couldn't possibly have left behind.

As we gradually unpacked the boxes and bags, their contents scrawled on the front in black marker pen, a feeling of familiarity began to settle around us.

As the days went on and with everything in their rightful place, we began to explore the area.

Within a stone's throw of our new home was an old church, rows, and rows of moss-laden graves. Some old and crumbled, long forgotten, others new, adorned with freshly placed flowers. At the back of the church a hidden worn path overgrown with weeds. Along a tree-lined woodland before the river came into view, clear and sparkling. Fields stretched for miles ahead, views of St Catherine's Hill in the distance. Not so different from the countryside around the cottage we had left behind.

Our garden was much smaller, and manageable, perfect for our new lifestyle.

There was a studio for Sandra to continue with her artwork that she had started while at the cottage. Having some success selling at craft fairs and exhibitions it was good for her to carry on. There was also a man-shed for me to sit in and ponder on our new, much slower pace of life. And so, we were set.

Each spring I set up breeding nets at the back of the garden to rear caterpillars into perfectly formed butterflies which I release into the wild. There is now an insect 'hotel' built from bamboo canes and pinned onto the fence. Holes have been cut into the fence as hedgehog runs. Also, a patch of ground where weeds are left to flourish, providing food and shelter for all sorts of tiny creatures.

You can take the man out of conservation, but you can never take conservation out of the man.

The children often visit; our grandchildren are now fast reaching adulthood, with the beginnings of independent lives. Our great-grandson, Reggie, is a much-loved new addition to the family.

Christmas remains a special time for all the family. With the bungalow fit to bursting I dust down the box of magic tricks to the sound of *'Granddad, no more magic tricks, we know how you do them.'*

With more time to spare I have rekindled my love for photography. I can often be found crawling through the undergrowth trying to capture the near perfect image of the many tiny creatures that I am still so fascinated by. Maybe the time has come to look for more earwigs. I wonder if Sandra has a spare teapot.

A Wife's Tale

'WOULD YOU LIKE TO COME OUT WITH ME TONIGHT?' asked Geoff, the very handsome boy next door.

As a young fifteen-year-old girl, I readily said yes and with great excitement began to plan what I was going to wear. I hoped I could make up my eyes in the very fashionable black eyeliner look without my dad noticing and insisting I wash it all off.

Dressed in a rather short mini skirt, high heel shoes with the obligatory pointed toes, which rendered them useless to walk in, I felt rather glamorous for my very first date. I wondered where he would take me. Maybe the cinema or a nice meal in the local café? Back then going out for a meal in a restaurant was only for the rich and famous.

The arranged time finally arrived. On hearing a knock at the door, I thought, here goes, I was about to enter the grown-up world of dating.

With suppressed excitement, not wanting to look too eager, I made my way unsteadily down the stone staircase leading out of the flats, holding tightly on to the banister, not wanting to stumble in my very grown-up shoes. I still wondered where we were going.

I was rather surprised when Geoff headed off into the direction of the bomb site.

'Thought I would show you the silkworms which have just hatched on the privet bush,' he said.

'That would be wonderful,' was my reply. I was trying hard not to show my disappointment.

With great excitement, on Geoff's part, and with me tottering over the rubble and stones, wondering if any minute I might break my ankle, we finally reached the bush containing the silkworm hatchings. For the next hour, and with great enthusiasm, Geoff explained the life circle of a silkworm.

'Would you like to come out with me again?' asked Geoff as he walked me back home.

Not being one to give up easily I said I would, wondering what delights were in store next time.

And so, it began.

Many dates later, after walks around the park, strolls round London Zoo after dark, listening to the wolves howling (now that really was a treat), I knew this was the real thing.

Looking five years on from that very first date.

We were now married and with two young children, Aron and Vincent; we found ourselves living in a fairly modern council flat on a truly diverse and large housing estate in Bermondsey, where we had both grown up.

With Geoff's wages being so low and with me being a stay-at-home mum for our two boys, there was little in the way of luxuries. We had to make our own entertainment by way of walks in any open green spaces we could find, Geoff explaining to us all, with great enthusiasm, the life cycle of the many insects found on the way. Memories of the silkworms often came to mind.

Geoff reached the ten-year milestone working at London Zoo and with our boys, and the addition of our baby daughter, Angela, we each realised London wasn't the place we wanted to bring up our young family.

We wanted to give the boys the freedom to run, build dens and not have to worry about the ever-increasing traffic in London, and the streets that now we felt were becoming unsafe to play in.

When a head keeper position came up at Marwell, we jumped at the chance, and very soon after that first interview, we found ourselves living in the country, and what an adventure that was.

An incredibly old cottage, run-down, but oozing character, came with the job. We soon made it our home and with lots of space for the boys to run in we readily adapted to country life.

With Geoff working such long hours five to seven days a week and sometimes not getting home until eight in the evening, depending on the rota, much of the work at home was left to me, although he did more than his fair share when he could.

As well as taking in orphaned animals we were also state registered short-term foster parents, giving a home to children who, for some reason or other, their parents were unable to look after, usually for short periods of time. One of the children arrived for three months and settled in so well. It was decided she would never be able to return to her birth parents so, she, in time, became our fourth child, Sylvia.

Life in the early days was hard. Geoff's wages were low so anything we needed we had to make ourselves or buy second hand. For many years, my birthday present in the autumn was two bags of coal, very necessary at the time.

Geoff and the children spent many an hour rooting through the woods looking for fallen tree branches to turn into logs for the fire, the smaller ones being chopped for kindling, Geoff turning a chore into an adventure for the children.

Early winter and as the first frosts settled on the tree branches. It was time to harvest the abundance of sloe berries adorning the trees in the field, ready to make our first attempt at sloe gin.

As the colourless liquid gradually turned rose pink, we thought the time was right to sample our wares. Forgetting we were drinking neat gin one glass turned into two and then three, the rest of the evening was something of a blur…but what a treat.

Christmas was always a special time for all our family. With extraordinarily little money to buy presents we always made sure the children had a good time. Evenings were spent with the whole family making decorations, the favourite being crackers made from toilet roll holders and crepe paper. There was no worries of health and safety then. If we were unable to buy the bangs for the middle, amid much laughter, we would all shout *bang* as we pulled them.

We collected holly laden with bright red berries from the surrounding woods to add to ivy leaves and pine cones ready to turn into garlands to adorn the fireplace.

Both my parents and Geoff's mum would make sure the children had lots of presents to unwrap on Christmas morning, really taking the financial pressure away from us.

Every Christmas morning, Mr and Mrs Knowles, the zoo's director and wife, would invite us to the Hall where there would be presents under the tree for the children and mince pies for adults.

Although the zoo was closed to the public on Christmas day the animals still had to be fed and watered with the keepers going in to work for three hours in the morning and then back in the afternoon to carry out the evening routine. Living on site Geoff always volunteered to be the one to go back in, giving his keepers the chance to spend the remainder of Christmas Day with their families and to avoid travelling again.

After lunch, presents open, crackers pulled, Geoff would make his way back to work, taking the boys with him to become honorary zookeepers, where they would help feed the animals and settle them for the night.

Christmas evening, we would play board games around the fire, some invented and made by Geoff; we never really understood the rules, but he meant well.

Magic tricks were Geoff's favourite and amid a chorus of 'Not again, Dad, we know how you do it,' he carried on, in Tommy Cooper style, to try to entertain us.

Part of our self-sufficiency quest was a rather large vegetable patch where we grew everything from potatoes to soft fruit. Although hard work it kept us in fresh produce all year round, with that and eggs from the chickens and milk from the goats our shopping bills were very low indeed.

As time went on, we discovered life outside of Marwell, often walking the three miles, across fields and through bridleways to join in the activities in the village. For many years we were part of the Owslebury drama group, with us all having parts in the two yearly productions, one being the pantomime, always great fun. As with most village productions the more mistakes made the funnier the audience found it and believe me there were many mistakes. Our prompt, the formidable, but wonderful character, Miss Hoff, very often nodded off to sleep at the precise moment you had forgotten your next line.

With the zoo attracting more visitors and Geoff's wages increasing we were able to afford our first car, a second-hand ex-police rover. A giant of a beast and with no power steering very heavy to handle. We could often be seen driving down the country lanes, children, and the odd animal, in the back. Taking the goat to be mated, always a cold wet autumn day, the goat with her head through the window bleating at passers-by. One of the children holding on to her so she didn't try to climb over the front seat. As I said no health and safety back then. A requirement, by law, was for our sheep to be dipped yearly to rid them of any parasites they may have. A local farmer Mike allowed us to use his dip. This meant leaving the country lanes for the main road and with two fully grown sheep on the back seat of the car, it was an interesting journey for us and other road users.

With the years rolling by and the children becoming more independent, our small holding became smaller until one day the field was empty. The goat sheds turned into log stores and a much quieter life for us... until... the children left home, got married and had children of their own and then it all started again.

First Lewis, our eldest grandchild, then along came Leah, closely followed by Bethany, Emily, James, Matthew, and finally Summer.

Camps rebuilt in the woodland, the field bursting into life again with the sound of children playing. There was the time a stray cat was found and carried up the path in a cardboard box, to be given a new home with us. Trips to the zoo after closing time, our Grandchildren now having a waiting list of friends wanting to come with them.

We had a wonderful, at times, chaotic lifestyle living in the country with Geoff doing his dream job. Times were hard, sometimes wondering how we were going to pay the next bill; there were arguments, but never long lasting. It was with some risk Geoff left a secure job at London Zoo, leaving our home, friends and family, but I have no doubt we did the right thing. Giving the children the opportunity to grow up with nature and freedom to run was the best decision we have ever made.

The Changing Role of Zoos

My own personal view

THROUGHOUT MY CAREER IN ZOOS, FIRSTLY, AT THE age of fifteen as a junior helper in the Insect House at London Zoo, up until retiring from my post as Head Keeper of the reptile and invertebrate section at Marwell Zoological Park in Hampshire some fifty years later, I have witnessed many changes in the way animals are cared for, in my opinion, all of them, for the better.

From the early days wild animals in zoos were kept in small-barred cages, packed together with little thought, or understanding for their wellbeing. They were there just to amuse the public, often being captured from the wild and placed in a cold sterile environment, with no thought to their natural habitat. This was not done out of carelessness, just lack of thought and understanding.

The joy I felt working in my dream job was sometimes overshadowed by the processes used to ensure continuity of exhibits. One that will always stay with me was the digging up of ant nests. Although we took every precaution possible to ensure minimum disruption, and with the queen ants staying low down in the nest and we knew the ants would work together to regenerate, I never felt completely comfortable with doing it.

I am so pleased that in the current climate taking any animal from the wild is not only unlawful, but it is also totally unnecessary.

As time went on the public demanded better conditions for captive animals along with more emphasis on animal welfare, bigger and better enclosures were built to mimic the natural environment of the individual species.

The role of zoos has changed dramatically over the years, specialising in many different areas of animal welfare, stringent record keeping, captive breeding and animal enrichment.

With conservation breeding programmes being co-ordinated among zoos and private animal collections, throughout the world some species of animal and insects have been brought back from the brink of extinction. Whether due to habitat loss or hunting by man some species have definitely been endangered to a limit that has been turned around by the intervention of captive breeding and protection.

At Marwell the Scimitar-horned Oryx, which is the original emblem of the zoo, is a classic example of this. Another success is the tiny Partula snail, as I mentioned in a previous chapter.

One of the challenges I faced when setting up the tropical house was how to furnish the exhibits to create a natural habitat for each individual species, while at the same time ensuring a good display for the public, with the emphasis on education and conservation.

I do hope I achieved this and went some way in inspiring the public to become involved in conservation, maybe starting with our own native species often found in their own gardens.

Science now plays a huge part in animal conservation. A prime example is the B.U.G.S, Biodiversity Underpinning Global Survival department at London Zoo which replaced the old insect house where I first started my career. Now it is a pinnacle in breeding endangered species with world-wide reintroduction programmes.

With keepers now working in state-of-the-art climate-controlled breeding rooms, things are a far cry from the cloying and musty rooms with little natural light where I spent much of my early working days.

Times really have changed for the better.

Education plays a particularly important role in the modern zoo, both London Zoo and Marwell Zoo boast the very best in education facilities. Modern classrooms and teachers ready to take on the challenges of teaching the numerous school parties that visit the zoo every day. Each school party keen to learn about the animals all around them. Budding zookeepers and conservationists in the making, teaching young minds the importance of our natural world, hoping one day it will make a difference is now key to the future and recognised as a major part in the zoo's role of existence.

Animal enrichment also plays an extremely important part in the wellbeing of zoo animals. To mimic the wild where animals must fend for themselves to survive, the keeping staffs devise ways of hiding food for the animals to hunt for. As if in the wild, this encourages and maintains their natural instinct. As well as creating a more natural environment the sight of an animal foraging for food is both entertaining and educational for the general public.

The creation of safari parks was a major step forward in wild animal management. The introduction of large secure areas for individual species to roam freely, while at the same time important conservation work can continue behind the scenes, was a substantial move forward.

The introduction of the Zoo Licensing Act 1981 was a turning point in ensuring the absolute best of conditions for both animals and employees within UK zoos.

Every four years a team of zoo directors, vets and government officials would arrive at the zoo, clip boards in hand, to inspect every aspect of animal welfare and public safety. Each individual enclosure would undergo a stringent examination. The condition of the animals, the sturdiness of the wire, the height of the overhang, the distance between the enclosure and the public barrier. Staff safety records and animal escape procedures, all checked. *No more almost the great escape!*

As a head keeper I was part of the trained gun team, on call should any animal escapes that could be a danger to life were reported. As part of the inspection, I once was asked random questions on training and procedure which I answered to the best of my ability. Best not mention the hackney thunderer whistle!

In 2002 the Zoo Licensing Act was amended to include conservation, education, and research. This was welcomed by many zoos both in the UK and EU.

Both London Zoo and Marwell are forerunners in the way zoos have evolved over the years. With fast dwindling natural habitats, both home and abroad, the destruction by man of the rainforest, and the effect of climate change having world-wide consequences, there has never been a more important role for the modern zoo.

For me one of the most positive aspects is the way zoos have evolved is the captive breeding of many species. What started for me as small individual programmes at London Zoo when I was beside myself with excitement to have successfully bred spiders and praying mantis, has now transformed into major captive breeding and reintroduction programmes. I am so proud of my own contribution to such programmes giving me the opportunity to breed extremely rare and extinct species.

But I could never forget how I first started, using Mother's best teapot and the amazing earwigs.

 Matador